THE UNIS CEMETERY AT SAQQARA

Volume I

THE TOMB OF IRUKAPTAH

The Australian Centre for Egyptology

Report 15

THE UNIS CEMETERY AT SAQQARA

Volume I

THE TOMB OF IRUKAPTAH

A. McFarlane

With contributions by
S. Shafik, E. Thompson, N. Victor

ISBN: 0-85668-818-5

Published in England by Aris and Phillips Ltd.,
Teddington House, Warminster,
Wiltshire BA12 8PQ

CONTENTS

PLATES

PREFACE AND ACKNOWLEDGEMENTS

The tomb of Irukaptah at Saqqara is among a number of rock-cut Old Kingdom tombs immediately south of the Unis causeway which were discovered by Abd el-Salam Mohammed Hussein in 1939-40 during excavations he undertook in that area (see *Pls. 5, 38a*). The work formed part of his research on pyramid complexes in the Memphite cemeteries, a brief report of which was published posthumously in *Proceedings of the Royal Society of Historical Studies* 1 [1952], 25-40. The causeway linking Unis' Valley Temple with his pyramid on the plateau 660 metres to the west was designed to make use of a natural ravine running east-west between two rock outcrops which probably served as a quarry during the construction of Djoser's Step Pyramid. The causeway was built up from the ground level and thus avoided the necessity of cutting a road through rock. In the course of this construction, dozens of tombs completed prior to the reign of Unis were obscured either by the causeway itself or by the resulting debris and later wind-blown sand. Presumably undisturbed since that time, those that have been excavated exhibit little structural damage and preserve much of their architectural and decorative features.

Well known as the 'Butcher's Tomb', the tomb of Irukaptah was investigated in 1956-57 by Boris de Rachewiltz and incompletely published in a small monograph, *The Rock Tomb of Irw-k3-Ptḥ* (Leiden, 1960). The distinctive characteristics of the tomb's architectural and decorative features have not previously received the attention they deserve. Rock tombs in the Memphite necropoli are not common and, frequently better preserved than constructed mastabas, require further study. Irukaptah's tomb, among the rare examples of rock-cut tombs at Saqqara, has sustained little structural damage and minimal deterioration of its relief decoration executed directly on the rock walls. While the quality of relief does not reflect the highest artistic standards of the late Fifth and early Sixth Dynasties, the wall scenes are of importance because of their unusual composition and the preservation of painted details. A prominent feature of the tomb's decoration is the extensive use of engaged statuary. No other rock-cut statues of the Old Kingdom, in the capital or in Upper Egypt, can compare with those of Irukaptah in the amount of colour and detail retained.

Previously excavated and subsequently conserved by the Inspectorate of Antiquities at Saqqara, the excavation work of the present expedition was limited to reclearing the burial apartments with the aim of recording their architectural features.

The primary purpose of the project has been to produce and publish a full record of the tomb of Irukaptah. This volume presents the architectural features in plans and sections, and the scenes and inscriptions in both facsimile drawings and in photographs. More than warranted by the amount of paint preserved in the tomb, some colour photographs are included to augment written information on the colour conventions. The text provides basic descriptions of the architecture and of each theme in the wall scenes, followed by short commentaries. An attempt has been made to compare significant aspects of the art and architecture with data from other near-contemporary tombs, but is not intended to be a full study. The engaged statues, an outstanding feature, are treated in a separate chapter, also with comparative comments. As a large portion of painted colour survives on both the wall decoration and the statues, the colour conventions are given in each sub-section of the wall scenes and individually for each statue; hieroglyphic signs are listed under "Decoration and Colour Conventions".

Abbreviations used in the text are, unless otherwise noted, as follows: H = maximum height; W = maximum width; D = maximum depth.

The undertaking of this project was made possible by a grant from the Australian Research Council, and this generous financial support is acknowledged with gratitude. My most sincere appreciation is extended to the Supreme Council of Antiquities for its valuable and significant cooperation throughout the course of the expedition's work in Egypt. In particular thanks are due to the Chairman, Professor Dr. Gaballa A. Gaballa, to the Head of the Central Administration of Antiquities for Cairo and Giza, Dr. Zahi Hawass, and to the Director of Antiquities at Saqqara, Mr. Mohamed Hagras, as well as to personnel of the Saqqara Inspectorate for providing every possible assistance.

Work in the tomb of Irukaptah was carried out over two seasons in 1997, August and November-December, and another in January-February 1999. The expedition was accompanied in the first two seasons by Inspector Mr. Mohamed Hendawy and in the third by Inspector Mr. Atif Omer. To each I would like to express deep appreciation of their unfailing cooperation and help during the fieldwork which greatly facilitated the successful completion of this project.

All who participated in the work on site and in the preparation of this report are particularly deserving of recognition, and it is a pleasure to acknowledge most gratefully their individual roles and contributions. The epigraphic work was achieved with assistance from Mr. Sameh Shafik (Sohag) who also inked the finely detailed line drawings for publication. Mr. Naguib Victor (Sydney) was responsible for measuring and recording all the architectural features and produced the architectural drawings of the tomb. The survey of the tomb and its surroundings was carried out by Mr. Allan Cavanagh (Newcastle) and the drawing of the survey section is the work of Ms. Helen Wilkins (Sydney). The photographs were provided by Mr. Nasser el-Din Abd el-Monem (Egyptian Museum Cairo), the late Mr. Hassaballa el-Tayeb (Saqqara) and Mr. Lyle van Leeuwen (Sydney). Mrs. Elizabeth Thompson (Macquarie University) prepared all the final artwork for this volume. Prof. Naguib Kanawati kindly read the manuscript with a welcome critical eye and Ms. Kim Wilson (Sydney) was responsible for the final editing and preparation of the text for publication.

Ann McFarlane

ABBREVIATIONS

Abu-Bakr, *Giza*: Abu-Bakr, A. M., *Excavations at Giza 1949-1950* (Cairo, 1953).

Actes XXIXe Congrès: *Actes du XXIXe Congrès internationale des Orientalistes, Egyptologie* (Paris, 1975).

Aegyptische Inschriften: *Aegyptische Inschriften aus den Königliche Museen zu Berlin*, ed. C. Roeder, 2 vols. (Berlin, 1901, 1924).

Altenmüller, *Mehu*: Altenmüller, H., *Die Wanddarstellungen im Grab des Mehu in Saqqara* (Mainz, 1998).

ASAE: *Annales du Service des Antiquités de l'Égypte.*

Badawy, *Iteti*: Badawy, A., *The Tombs of Iteti, Sekhemʿankh-Ptah, and Kaemnofert at Giza* (Berkeley, 1976).

Badawy, *Nyhetep-Ptah*: Badawy, A., *The Tomb of Nyhetep-Ptah at Giza and the Tomb of ʿAnkhmʿahor at Saqqara* (Berkeley, 1978).

Baer, *Rank and Title*: Baer, K., *Rank and Title in the Old Kingdom: The Structure of the Egyptian Administration in the Fifth and Sixth Dynasties* (Chicago, 1960).

Barta, *Opferliste*: Barta, W., *Die altägyptische Opferliste von der Frühzeit bis zur griechisch-römischen Epoche* (Berlin, 1963).

Begelsbacher-Fischer, *Götterwelt des Alten Reiches*: Begelsbacher-Fischer, B. L., *Untersuchungen zur Götterwelt des Alten Reiches im Spiegel der Privatgräber der IV. und V. Dynastie* (Göttingen, 1981).

BIFAO: *Bulletin de l'Institut Français d'Archéologie Orientale du Caire.*

von Bissing, *Gem-ni-kai*: von Bissing, F. W., *Die Mastaba des Gem-ni-kai*, 2 vols. (Berlin, 1905, 1911).

Blackman, *Meir*: Blackman, A. M., *The Rock Tombs of Meir*, 6 vols. (London, 1914-53).

Borchardt, *Ne-user-Reʿ*: Borchardt, L., *Das Grabdenkmal des Königs Ne-user-Reʿ* (Leipzig, 1907; repr. Osnabrück, 1984).

Borchardt, *Sa3ḥu-Reʿ*: Borchardt, L., *Das Grabdenkmal des Königs Sa3ḥu-Reʿ*, 2 vols. (Leipzig, 1910, 1913; repr. Osnabrück, 1981-82).

Borchardt, *Statuen*: Borchardt, L., *Statuen und Statuetten von Königen und Privatleuten* (Cat. gén. du Musée du Caire), 5 vols. (Cairo, 1911-36).

Borchardt, *Denkmäler*: Borchardt, L., *Denkmäler des Alten Reiches* (Cat. gén. du Musée du Caire), 2 vols. (Cairo, 1937, 1964).

Boreaux, *Nautique*: Boreaux, C., *Ètudes de nautique Ègyptienne: l'art de la navigation en Ègypte jusque à le fin de l'Ancien Empire* (Cairo, 1924-25).

Brewer - Friedman, *Fish and Fishing*: Brewer, D. J. - Friedman, R. F., *Fish and Fishing in Ancient Egypt* (Warminster, 1989).

Brewer et al., *Plants and Animals*: Brewer, D. J., - Redford, D. B., - Redford, S., *Domestic Plants and Animals: The Egyptian Origins* (Warminster, 1994).

Capart, *Rue de tombeaux*: Capart, J., *Une rue de tombeaux à Saqqarah*, 2 vols. (Brussels, 1907).

Cherpion, *Mastabas et hypogées*: Cherpion, N., *Mastabas et hypogées d'Ancien Empire: le problème de la datation* (Brussels, 1989).

Chron. d'Ég.: *Chronique d'Égypte.*

Critères de datation: *Les Critères de datation stylistiques à l'Ancien Empire*, ed. N. Grimal (Cairo, 1998).

Curto, *Gli scavi*: Curto, S., *Gli scavi italiani a el-Ghiza (1903)* (Rome, 1963).

Darby et al., *Food*: Darby, W. J. - Ghalioungui, P. - Grivetti, L., *Food, The Gift of Osiris* (London, 1977).

Davies, *Ptahhetep*: Davies, N. de G., *The Mastaba of Ptahhetep and Akhethetep at Saqqarah*, 2 vols. (London, 1900-1901).

Davies, *Sheikh Saïd*: Davies, N. de G., *The Rock Tombs of Sheikh Saïd* (London, 1901).

Davies, *Deir el-Gebrâwi*: Davies, N. de G., *The Rock Tombs of Deir el-Gebrâwi*, 2 vols. (London, 1902).

von Droste, *Der Igel*: von Droste zu Hülshoff, V., *Der Igel im Alten Ägypten* (Hildesheim, 1980).

Duell, *Mereruka*: Duell, P., *The Mastaba of Mereruka*, 2 vols. (Chicago, 1938).

Dunham, *Naga-ed-Dêr*: Dunham, D., *Naga-ed-Dêr Stelae of the First Intermediate Period* (London, 1937).

Dunham - Simpson, *Mersyankh III*: Dunham, D. - Simpson, W. K., *The Mastaba of Queen Mersyankh III: G7530-7540* (Boston, 1974).

Eaton-Krauss, *Statuary*: Eaton-Krauss, M., *The Representations of Statuary in Private Tombs of the Old Kingdom* (Wiesbaden, 1984).

Egyptian Art: *Egyptian Art in the Age of the Pyramids, Catalogue Metropolitan Museum of Art* (New York, 1999).
Épron - Wild, *Ti*: Épron, L. - Wild, H., *Le tombeau de Ti*, 3 fascs. (Cairo, 1939-66).
Fazzini, *Images for Eternity*: Fazzini, R., *Images for Eternity: Egyptian Art from Berkeley and Brooklyn* (New York, 1975).
Festschrift Edel: *Festschrift Elmar Edel, 12. März 1979*, eds. M. Görg - E. Pusch (Bamberg, 1979).
Firth - Gunn, *Teti Pyr. Cem.*: Firth, C. M. - Gunn, B., *Teti Pyramid Cemeteries*, 2 vols. (Cairo, 1926).
Fischer, *Varia*: Fischer, H. G., *Egyptian Studies I: Varia* (New York, 1976).
Fischer, *Varia Nova*: Fischer, H. G., *Varia Nova* (New York, 1996).
Followers of Horus: *The Followers of Horus: Studies dedicated to Michael Allen Hoffman*, eds. R. Friedman - B. Adams (Oxford, 1992).
GM: *Göttinger Miszellen: Beiträge zur ägyptologischen Diskussion.*
Griffith, *Kahun and Gurob*: *The Petrie Papyri: hieratic papyri from Kahun and Gurob*, ed. F. L. Griffith (London, 1898).
Hannig, *Handwörterbuch*: Hannig, R., *Die Sprache der Pharaonen: Grosses Handwörterbuch Ägyptich-Deutch* (Mainz, 1995).
Harpur, *Decoration*: Harpur, Y., *Decoration in Egyptian Tombs of the Old Kingdom: Studies in Orientation and Scene Content* (London, 1987).
Hassan, *Gîza*: Hassan, S., *Excavations at Gîza*, 10 vols. (Oxford/Cairo, 1929-60).
Hassan, *Saqqara*: Hassan, S., *Excavations at Saqqara*, 3 vols., ed. Z. Iskander (Cairo, 1975).
Hayes, *Scepter*: Hayes, W. C., *The Scepter of Egypt*, 2 vols. (New York, 1959).
Helck, *Beamtentitel*: Helck, W., *Untersuchungen zu den Beamtentiteln des ägyptischen Alten Reiches* (Glückstadt, 1954).
Hommages Leclant: *Hommages à Jean Leclant*, 4 vols. (Cairo, 1994).
Ikram, *Choice Cuts*: Ikram, S., *Choice Cuts: meat production in ancient Egypt* (Leuven, 1995).
James, *Khentika*: James, T. G. H., *The Mastaba of Khentika Called Ikhekhi* (London, 1953).
James, *Hieroglyphic Texts*: James, T. G. H., *Hieroglyphic Texts from Egyptian Stelae, etc., in the British Museum*, vol. 1 (London, 1961).
JAOS: *Journal of the American Oriental Society.*
JARCE: *Journal of the American Research Center in Egypt.*
JEA: *Journal of Egyptian Archaeology.*
Jéquier, *Particuliers*: Jéquier, G., *Tombeaux de particuliers contemporains de Pepi II* (Cairo, 1929).
Jones, *Boats*: Jones, D., *Boats* (London, 1995).
Junker, *Gîza*: Junker, H., *Grabungen auf dem Friedhof des Alten Reiches bei den Pyramiden von Gîza*, 12 vols. (Vienna, 1929-55).
Kanawati, *Egyptian Administration*: Kanawati, N., *The Egyptian Administration in the Old Kingdom: Evidence on its Economic Decline* (Warminster, 1977).
Kanawati, *El-Hawawish*: Kanawati, N., *The Rock Tombs of El-Hawawish: The Cemetery of Akhmim*, 10 vols. (Sydney, 1980-1992).
Kanawati, *A Mountain Speaks*: Kanawati, N., *A Mountain Speaks: The First Australian Excavations in Egypt* (Sydney, 1988).
Kanawati, *El-Hagarsa*: Kanawati, N., *The Tombs of El-Hagarsa*, 3 vols. (Sydney, 1993-95).
Kanawati - Abder-Raziq, *Teti Cemetery* 3: Kanawati, N. - Abder-Raziq, M., *The Teti Cemetery at Saqqara*, vol. 3: *The Tombs of Neferseshemre and Seankhuiptah* (Warminster, 1998).
Kanawati - Abder-Raziq, *Teti Cemetery* 5: Kanawati, N. - Abder-Raziq, M., *The Teti Cemetery at Saqqara*, vol. 5: *The Tomb of Hesi* (Warminster, 1999).
Kanawati - Abder-Raziq, *Teti Cemetery* 6: Kanawati, N. - Abder-Raziq, M., *The Teti Cemetery at Saqqara*, vol. 6: *The Tomb of Nikauisesi* (Warminster, 2000).
Kanawati - Hassan, *Teti Cemetery* 1: Kanawati, N. - Hassan, A., *The Teti Cemetery at Saqqara*, vol. 1: *The Tombs of Nedjet-em-pet, Ka-aper and Others* (Sydney, 1996).
Kanawati - Hassan, *Teti Cemetery* 2: Kanawati, N. - Hassan, A., *The Teti Cemetery at Saqqara*, vol. 2: *The Tomb of Ankhmahor* (Warminster, 1997).
Kanawati - McFarlane, *Akhmim* 1: Kanawati, N. - McFarlane, A., *Akhmim in the Old Kingdom: I Chronology and Administration* (Sydney, 1992).
Kanawati - McFarlane, *Deshasha*: Kanawati, N. - McFarlane, A., *Deshasha: The Tombs of Inti, Shedu and Others* (Sydney, 1993).
Kanawati et al., *Saqqara* 1: Kanawati, N. - El-Khouli, A. - McFarlane, A. - Maksoud, N. V., *Excavations at Saqqara: North-West of Teti's Pyramid*, vol. 1 (Sydney, 1984).
Kaplony, *Methethi*: Kaplony, P., *Studien zum Grab des Methethi* (Bern, 1976).
El-Khouli - Kanawati, *Quseir el-Amarna*: El-Khouli, A. - Kanawati, N., *Quseir el-Amarna: The Tombs of Pepy-ankh and Khewen-wekh* (Sydney, 1989).
El-Khouli - Kanawati, *El-Hammamiya*: El-Khouli, A. - Kanawati, N., *The Old Kingdom Tombs of El-Hammamiya* (Sydney, 1990).

LÄ: *Lexikon der Ägyptologie*, eds. W. Helck - E. Otto - W. Westendorf (Wiesbaden, 1972-).
Landström, *Ships*: Landström, B., *Ships of the Pharaohs: 4000 years of Egyptian shipbuilding* (New York, 1970).
Lapp, *Opferformel*: Lapp, G., *Die Opferformel des Alten Reiches* (Mainz/Rhein, 1986).
Lepsius, *Denkmäler*: Lepsius, C. R., *Denkmäler aus Ägypten und Äthiopien*, 12 vols. (Berlin, 1849-59).
Lepsius, *Ergänzungsband*: Lepsius, C. R., *Denkmäler aus Ägypten und Äthiopien, Ergänzungsband* (Leipzig, 1913).
Lloyd et al., *Saqqâra Tombs* 2: Lloyd, A. B. - Spencer, A. J. - El-Khouli, A., *Saqqâra Tombs II: The Mastabas of Meru, Semdenti, Khui and Others* (London, 1990).
Mackay et al., *Hemamieh*: Mackay, E. G. H. - Harding, L. - Petrie, W. M. F., *Bahrein and Hemamieh* (London, 1929).
Macramallah, *Idout*: Macramallah, R., *Le mastaba d'Idout* (Cairo, 1935).
Mariette, *Mastabas*: Mariette, A., *Les mastabas de l'Ancien Empire* (Paris, 1889).
Martin, *Hetepka*: Martin, G. T., *The Tomb of Hetepka and other Reliefs and Inscriptions from the Sacred Animal Necropolis, North Saqqara 1964-73* (London, 1979).
Maspero, *Trois années de fouilles*: Maspero, G., *Trois années de fouilles dans les tombeaux de Thebes et de Memphis* (Paris, 1884).
MDAIK: *Mitteilungen des Deutschen Archäologischen Instituts Abteilung Kairo.*
Mekhitarian, *Painting*: Mekhitarian, A., *Egyptian Painting* (Geneva, 1978).
MMJ: *The Metropolitan Museum Journal.*
Mogensen, *Mastaba egyptién*: Mogensen, M., *Le mastaba egyptién de la Glyptotèque Ny Carlsberg* (Copenhagen, 1921).
Mohr, *Hetep-her-akhti*: Mohr, H. T., *The Mastaba of Hetep-her-akhti. Study of an Egyptian tomb chapel in the Museum of antiquities* (Leiden, 1943).
Montet, *Vie privée*: Montet, P., *Scènes de la vie privée dans les tombeaux égyptiens de l'Ancien Empire* (Strasbourg, 1925).
de Morgan, *Catalogue des monuments*: Morgan, J. de, *Catalogue des monuments et inscriptions de l'Égypte antique*, 3 vols. (Vienna, 1894-1909).
de Morgan, *Dahchour*: Morgan, J. de, *Fouilles à Dahchour,* 2 vols. (Vienna, 1895, 1903).
Moussa - Altenmüller, *Nefer*: Moussa, A. - Altenmüller, H., *The Tomb of Nefer and Ka-hay* (Mainz/Rhein, 1971).
Moussa - Altenmüller, *Nianchchnum*: Moussa, A. - Altenmüller, H., *Das Grab des Nianchchnum und Chnumhotep* (Mainz/Rhein, 1977).
Moussa - Junge, *Two Craftsmen*: Moussa, A. - Junge, F., *Two Tombs of Craftsmen* (Mainz/Rhein, 1975).
Munro, *Unas-Friedhof*: Munro, P., *Der Unas-Friedhof Nord-west* (Mainz, 1993).
Murray, *Saqqara*: Murray, M., *Saqqara Mastabas*, 2 vols. (London, 1905, 1937).
Myśliwiec, *Nowe oblicza Sakkary*: Myśliwiec, K., *Nowe oblicza Sakkary* (Warsaw, 1999).
Or.: *Orientalia, Nova Series.*
Paget - Pirie, *Ptah-hetep*: Paget, R. F. E. - Pirie, A. A. - Griffith, F. L., *The Tomb of Ptah-hetep* (London, 1898).
Petrie - Murray, *Memphite Chapels*: Petrie, H. - Murray, M., *Seven Memphite Tomb Chapels* (London, 1952).
Petrie, *Deshasheh*: Petrie, W. M. F., *Deshasheh 1897* (London, 1898).
Petrie, *Dendereh*: Petrie, W. M. F., *Dendereh 1898* (London, 1900).
Petrie, *Gizeh and Rifeh*: Petrie, W. M. F., *Gizeh and Rifeh* (London, 1907).
PM: Porter, B. - Moss, R., *Topographical Bibliography of Ancient Egyptian Hieroglyphic Texts, Reliefs and Paintings* (Oxford, 1927-52; second ed. J. Málek, 1960-).
Posener-Kriéger, *Archives d'Abousir*: Posener-Kriéger, P., *Les archives du temple funéraire de Néferirkarê-Kakaï, les papyrus d'Abousir*, 2 vols. (Cairo, 1976).
Quibell, *Saqqara* 1: Quibell, J. E., *Excavations at Saqqara 1905-1906*, vol. 1 (Cairo, 1907).
Quibell, *Saqqara* 3: Quibell, J. E., *Excavations at Saqqara 1907-1908*, vol. 3 (Cairo, 1909).
Quibell, *Hesy*: Quibell, J. E., *Excavations at Saqqara 1911-1912*, vol. 5: *The Tomb of Hesy* (Cairo, 1913).
de Rachewiltz, *Irw-k3-Ptḥ*: Rachewiltz, B. de, *The Rock Tomb of Irw-k3-Ptḥ* (Leiden, 1960).
Ranke, *Personennamen*: Ranke, H., *Die altägyptischen Personennamen*, 3 vols. (Glückstadt, 1935-77).
Reisner, *Tomb Development*: Reisner, G. A., *The Development of the Egyptian Tomb down to the Accession of Cheops* (Cambridge MA, 1936).
Reisner, *Giza*: Reisner, G. A., *A History of the Giza Necropolis*, vol. 1 (Cambridge MA, 1942).
Roth, *Palace Attendants*: Roth, A. M., *A Cemetery of Palace Attendants, including G 2084-2099 G 2230 + 2231 and G 2240* (Boston, 1995).
SAK: *Studien zur Altägyptischen Kultur.*
Saleh, *Tombs at Thebes*: Saleh, M., *Three Old Kingdom Tombs at Thebes* (Mainz/Rhein, 1977).

Saleh - Sourouzian, *Museum Cairo*: Saleh, M. - Sourouzian, H., *Official Catalogue: The Egyptian Museum Cairo* (Mainz, 1987).
Säve-Söderbergh, *Hamra Dom*: Säve-Söderbergh, T., *The Old Kingdom Cemetery at Hamra Dom (el-Qasr wa es-Saiyed)* (Stockholm, 1994).
Schürmann, *Ii-nefret*: Schürmann, W., *Die Reliefs aus dem Grab des Pyramiden-vorstehers Ii-nefret: Eine Bilddokumentation des Badischen Landesmuseums Karlsruhe* (Karlsruhe, 1983).
Simpson, *Qar and Idu*: Simpson, W. K., *The Mastabas of Qar and Idu: G7101 and 7102* (Boston, 1976).
Simpson, *Sekhem-ankh-Ptah*: Simpson, W. K., *The Offering Chapel of Sekhem-ankh-Ptah in the Museum of Fine Arts, Boston* (Boston, 1976).
Simpson, *Kawab*: Simpson, W. K., *The Mastabas of Kawab, Khafkhufu I and II* (Boston, 1978).
Simpson, *Western Cemetery*: Simpson, W. K., *Mastabas of the Western Cemetery*: Part I (Boston, 1980).
Simpson, *Kayemnofret*: Simpson, W. K., *The Offering Chapel of Kayemnofret in the Museum of Fine Arts, Boston* (Boston, 1992).
Smith, *HESPOK*: Smith, W. S., *A History of Egyptian Sculpture and Painting in the Old Kingdom* (London, 1946).
Staehelin, *Tracht*: Staehelin, E., *Untersuchungen zur ägyptischen Tracht im Alten Reich* (Berlin, 1966).
Steindorff, *Catalogue Walters*: Steindorff, G., *Catalogue of the Egyptian Sculpture in the Walters Art Gallery* (Baltimore MD, 1946).
Strudwick, *Administration*: Strudwick, N., *The Administration of Egypt in the Old Kingdom* (London, 1985).
Studies Dunham: *Studies in Ancient Egypt, the Aegean and the Sudan: Essays in honor of Dows Dunham on the occasion of his 90th birthday, June 1, 1980*, eds. W. K. Simpson - W. M. Davis (Boston, 1981).
Studies Simpson: *Studies in Honor of William Kelly Simpson*, ed. P. de Manuelian, 2 vols. (Boston, 1996).
Vandier, *Mo^calla*: Vandier, J., *Mo^calla: La tombe d'Ankhtifi et la tombe de Sébekhotep* (Cairo, 1950).
Vandier, *Manuel*: Vandier, J., *Manuel d'archéologie égyptienne*, 6 vols. (Paris, 1952-78).
Varille, *Ni-ankh-Pepi*: Varille, A., *La tombe de Ni-ankh-Pepi à Zaouyet El-Mayetîn* (Cairo, 1938).
van de Walle, *Neferirtenef*: van de Walle, B., *La chapelle funéraire de Neferirtenef* (Brussels, 1978).
Verner, *Ptahshepses*: Verner, M., *Abusir, vol. I: The Mastaba of Ptahshepses* (Prague, 1977).
Verner, *Forgotten Pharaohs*: Verner, M., *Forgotten Pharaohs, Lost Pyramids: Abusir* (Prague, 1994).
Wb.: *Wörterbuch der ägyptischen Sprache*, eds. A. Erman, - H. Grapow, 6 vols. (Leipzig, 1926-31; new ed. 1971).
Weeks, *Cemetery G 6000*: Weeks, K., *Mastabas of Cemetery G 6000: Including G 6010 (Neferbauptah); G 6020 (Iymery); G 6030 (Ity); G 6040 (Shepseskafankh)* (Boston, 1994).
Wiebach, *Scheintür*: Wiebach, S., *Die ägyptische Scheintür* (Hamburg, 1981).
Wilkinson, *Garden*: Wilkinson, A., *The Garden in Ancient Egypt* (London, 1998).
Williams, *Perneb*: Williams, C., *The Decoration of the Tomb of Per-neb: The Technique and Color Conventions* (New York, 1932).
Wilson, *Food and Drink*: Wilson, H., *Egyptian Food and Drink* (Aylesbury, 1988).
Wreszinski, *Atlas*: Wreszinski, W., *Atlas zur altägyptischen Kulturgeschichte,* 2 cases (Leipzig, 1923-35; repr. Geneva, 1988).
Ziegler, *Catalogue des stèles*: Ziegler, C., *Catalogue des stèles, peintures et reliefs égyptiens de l'Ancien Empire et de la Première Période Intermédiaire* (Paris, 1990).
Ziegler, *Akhethetep*: Ziegler, C., *Le Mastaba d'Akhethetep: Une chapelle funèraire de l'Ancien Empire* (Paris, 1993).
Ziegler, *Statues*: Ziegler, C., *Les Statues égyptien de la Ancien Empire* (Paris, 1997).

THE TOMB OF IRUKAPTAH

I THE TOMB OWNER, HIS FAMILY AND DEPENDENTS

Tomb Owner

NAME

1- *Jrw-kꜣ-Ptḥ*[1] 'Irukaptah'. The name is written or except for a single instance in the form on the right jamb of the false door.[2]

2- *Ḫnw*[3] 'Khenu'. This name appears only on the upper and lower lintels and the left jamb of the false door.

TITLES and EPITHETS

1- *wʿb nswt* 'royal *wʿb*-priest'.[4]
2- *rḫ nswt* 'royal acquaintance'.[5]
3- *qbḥ nmt ʿbw-r nswt* 'libationer and butcher of the king's repast'. Although the translation of *qbḥ nmt* as 'master butcher'[6] is generally accepted, it would here seem preferable to take each word as separate but complementary titles. The two elements occur individually in titles on piers between the statue niches on the east wall, written twice as *nmt ʿbw-r nswt* 'butcher of the king's repast' and once as *qbḥ ʿbw-r nswt* 'libationer of the king's repast'.[7] Different forms also appear on the false door, without honorific transposition on the lower lintel and simply as *qbḥ nmt* on the left jamb. The reading of as *jʿw-r nswt*, traditionally interpreted as 'king's breakfast',[8] has been questioned with

---

1 Ranke, *Personennamen* 1, 40:22.
2 I am most grateful to Prof. H. Goedicke for providing me with hand copies he made in 1957 of inscriptions in this tomb. Fortunately, these texts include the writing of the owner's name from two of the piers between the statue niches, none of which are complete today.
3 Ranke, *Personennamen* 1, 270:4.
4 A religious office generally attested for officials who are not of the higher ranks and frequently held in association with *rḫ nswt* (Strudwick, *Administration*, 283).
5 Helck, *Beamtentitel*, 26; Brunner, *SAK* 1 [1974], 55-60; Fischer, *Varia*, 8 n.15.
6 Fischer, *Or.* 29 [1960], 171-77; Moussa - Junge, *Two Craftsmen*, 33; *Wb.* 5, 27:11. For 'butcher of the slaughterhouse' see Junker, *Gîza* 10, 124-25.
7 See Hannig, *Handwörterbuch*, 412; and for *djt qbḥw* as 'presenting a libation', Simpson, *Kawab*, 16, fig. 32. For a reading of 'butcher of the king's repast' see Moussa - Altenmüller, *Nefer*, 10, n.7.
8 Hassan, *Gîza* 3, 57, 60, 64, 67; vol. 9, 21-23; James, *Khentika*, 42; Moussa - Junge, *Two Craftsmen*, 34, 46; Kanawati et al., *Saqqara* 1, 15; Kanawati - Hassan, *Teti Cemetery* 1, 70; vol. 2, 13; also *Wb.* 1, 39:23.

justification by de Meulenaere whose suggestion of *ꜥbw-r nswt* 'king's repast'[9] appears to be valid.[10]

4- *qbḥ nmt pr-ꜥꜣ* 'libationer and butcher of the palace'.[11] The title is written with the determinative on the north wall, in front of the seated tomb owner at the north end of the east wall and all four examples on the false door, but not on the piers between the statues, where it may have been omitted to save space.
5- *jmꜣḫ(w)* 'the honoured one'.
6- *jmꜣḫ(w) ḫr Ptḥ rsj jnb.f* 'the honoured one before Ptah south of his wall'.
7- *jmꜣḫ(w) ẖr nṯr ꜥꜣ* 'the honoured one before the great god'.

Jrw-kꜣ-Ptḥ's functional role as 'libationer and butcher' is based on the term *qbḥ nmt*. Compounded in all but one inscription in his tomb with either *pr-ꜥꜣ* or *ꜥbw-r nswt*, such titles are not common in the Old Kingdom. Virtually all known holders of *qbḥ nmt* are attested in the Memphite cemeteries and dated between early Dynasty 5 and early Dynasty 6.[12] In this period and divided equally between Saqqara and Giza are attested some eighteen examples of the title, half in the simple form *qbḥ nmt* and half with the addition of *pr-ꜥꜣ*, which does not appear before the reign of Neuserre.[13]

The term *ꜥbw-r* regularly appears in offering lists as an item signifying a meal.[14] While the phrase *ꜥbw-r nswt* does not occur in menu lists, it is incorporated in a variety of offices held in the Old Kingdom, apparently exclusively at Memphis, by both senior and mid-low ranking officials.[15] None of the nearly two dozen known holders are dated earlier than mid-Dynasty 5 or later than mid-Dynasty 6. The titles of these tomb owners are *jmj-r ꜥbw-r (nb) nswt*,[16] often with the addition of *m*

---

9 *BIFAO* 81 Suppl. [1981], 87-89. Use of the sign is largely restricted to the Old Kingdom and Dynasty 26, and the four cited examples of phonetic spelling from offering lists confirm a reading of *ꜥb* or *ꜥb-r*. See also Junker, *Gîza* 2, 171; *Wb.* 1, 175:19.

10 Dorman, *Hommages Leclant* 1, 456-57; Darnell, *JEA* 75 [1989], 219 n.2; Fischer, *Varia Nova*, 32-33; Goedicke, *Studies Simpson* 1, 357. Barta has included both readings in his Dynasty 5 lists (*Opferliste*, 58, 74).

11 Hannig translates 'he who offers for the slaughtering in the great house' (*Handwörterbuch*, 412).

12 A single instance of *qbḥ nmt* in Upper Egypt at Naga ed-Deir is traditionally dated to the First Intermediate Period (Dunham, *Naga ed-Dêr*, no. 48). However, the fact that the title appears to be restricted to the period prior to mid-Dynasty 6 may lend weight to an earlier date (refer to recent proposed dating of Naga ed-Deir officials in Kanawati - McFarlane, *Akhmim* 1, 55-61, 265-69).

13 For a discussion of these titles with a list of holders, the first perhaps as early as Dynasty 3, see Fischer, *Or.* 29 [1960], 171-78. Three examples may be added, one of *qbḥ nmt* (Moussa - Junge, *Two Craftsmen*, ill. 4) and one of *qbḥ nmt pr-ꜥꜣ* (ibid, ill. 3, pls. 12, 14), as well as an unusual form, *qbḥw pr-ꜥꜣ* (Moussa - Altenmüller, *Nefer*, 10).

14 Barta, *Opferliste*, 48, 58, 74; Dorman, *Hommages Leclant* 1, 457.

15 These Old Kingdom titles and their holders are discussed by Dorman, *Hommages Leclant* 1, 458-62. To his list may be added two officials mentioned in the text above, *Jrj.n-kꜣ-Ptḥ* and *Jrw-kꜣ-Ptḥ*, and six others whose names are given in parentheses in the following note.

16 Barsanti, *ASAE* 1 [1900], figs. 9, 12; Épron - Wild, *Ti* 1, pl. 36; Jéquier, *Particuliers*, 110, fig. 124; James, *Khentika*, 42, pl. 7 (*Ḫntj-kꜣ.j/Jḫḫj*); Strudwick, *Administration*, 73 (*ꜥnḫ-m-ꜥ-Rꜥ*); Lloyd et al., *Saqqâra Tombs* 2, pl. 25 (*ꜥnḫ*); Kanawati - Hassan, *Teti Cemetery* 1, pls. 35, 65 (*Grf/Jtj*); vol. 2, pls. 22, 62; vol. 3, pls. 18, 58 (*Nfr-sšm-Rꜥ*); Fischer, *Varia Nova*, 40 pl. 6 (*Ḥtp-n.j*); Altenmüller, *Mehu*, 63-65, 221, 231, pls. 81, 86 (*Mrjj-Rꜥ-ꜥnḫ*).

swt.f nbt,[17] *jmj-r šnꜥ ꜥbw-r nswt (pr ꜥꜣ)*,[18] *ḥrj-sštꜣ n ꜥbw-r (nb) nswt pr-ꜥꜣ*.[19] In addition to *Jrw-kꜣ-Ptḥ*'s office of *qbḥ nmt ꜥbw-r nswt*, two other unique titles are known from another tomb south of Unis' causeway. The owner, *Jrj.n-kꜣ-Ptḥ*, bore *jmj-r ꜥḏ-(jḥ) ꜥbw-r nswt* 'overseer of the beef fat(?) of the king's repast'.[20] On an offering table found in his tomb but presumably inscribed for another similarly-named official, *Jrw-kꜣ-Ptḥ*, is *qbḥ nmt pr-ꜥꜣ ꜥbw-r nswt* which Moussa - Junge translate as 'the master butcher of the palace (for?) the breakfast of the king'.[21] The last is the only title known comparable to that held by *Jrw-kꜣ-Ptḥ/Ḫnw*. While the two butchers are near contemporaries, it is questionable whether the owner of the offering table, whose name is written 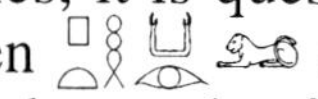 and who also bears *jmj-r ꜥḏ-(jḥ)* which is mentioned nowhere in the tomb of *Jrw-kꜣ-Ptḥ/Ḫnw*, can be identified with *Jrw-kꜣ-Ptḥ/Ḫnw*, as tentatively suggested by the excavators.[22] The vast majority of all these titles are attested at Saqqara and placed between the reigns of Neuserre and Pepy I.

Roth has remarked on the concentration in the Unis Cemetery of tombs belonging to royal butchers,[23] four adjacent to the causeway towards the end of Dynasty 5 and another early in Dynasty 6. It should also be noted that, while documented three times in the Unis Cemetery, the title 'overseer of the king's repast' is attested for six officials buried in the Teti Cemetery early in Dynasty 6.

It is interesting that titles formed with *ꜥbw-r nswt* and *qbḥ nmt pr ꜥꜣ*, as well as *jmj-r šnwtj*, appear in mid-Dynasty 5 at the time that major administrative reforms opened the bureaucracy to individuals with no connections to the royal family.[24] Strudwick mentions *jmj-r ꜥbw-r nswt* in his discussion of the department of granaries among a number of offices concerned with food supply,[25] but its exact interpretation is uncertain. The term *ꜥbw-r nswt* occurs in a fragmentary title preserved in the Abusir Papyri.[26] Dorman has proposed that the provisioning may be associated with a meal prepared not for presentation to the king himself, but to be offered by or on behalf of the king in a ritual context, a connection with temple and royal cults suggested by the use of *nb* and *m swt.f nbt*.[27] Perhaps the element *qbḥ* 'libation' is intended to distinguish a butcher with specific ritual duties from those commonly designated in the Old Kingdom as *sšm*.

---

17 Barsanti, *ASAE* 1 [1900], fig. 10; Hassan, *Saqqara* 3, figs. 40-41; Mariette, *Mastabas*, 185, 229; Kanawati et al., *Saqqara* 1, pls. 5-6.

18 Hassan, *Gîza* 3, figs. 54, 56, 58, pls. 21:1, 23-24; vol. 9, 21-23, pls. 6, 7A; Martin, *Hetepka*, 31, pl. 31 (No. 73). For a woman holding *sḥḏ šnꜥ ꜥbw-r nswt* see *Aegyptische Inschriften* 1, 67.

19 Borchardt, *Ne-user-Reꜥ*, 137; Kanawati et al., *Saqqara* 1, pls. 5-6.

20 Moussa - Junge, *Two Craftsmen*, 34, ill. 3, pl. 12. See also *sḥḏ rtḥ.w ꜥbw-r nswt* 'inspector of bakers of the king's repast' (Petrie, *Gizeh and Rifeh*, pl. 7A).

21 *Two Craftsmen*, 46, ill. 4.

22 Ibid, 46.

23 *JARCE* 25 [1988], 208-209, fig. 10.

24 Helck, *Beamtentitel*, 58; Baer, *Rank and Title*, 300; Strudwick, *Administration*, 337-38.

25 Ibid, 256, 259.

26 Posener - Kriéger, *Archives d'Abousir* 2, 608.

27 *Hommages Leclant* 1, 465-66. Dorman suggests the Old Kingdom titles may reflect participation in the reversion offerings of temple and mortuary cults, for which see Weeks, *Chron. d'Ég.* 58 [1983], 5-22, esp. 20-22.

Wife of Irukaptah

No name or titles accompany the two female figures depicted in the tomb, but both are in all likelihood the tomb owners' wife. One figure appears in the fowling scene sketched on the east wall, standing in the boat directly in front of the tomb owner and holding a bird. Among the four engaged statues on the west wall is that of a female who is almost the same height as the three male figures which probably represent *Jrw-kꜣ-Ptḥ*.

The Son(s?) of Irukaptah

NAME

Ptḥ-špss[28] 'Ptahshepses'. At the bottom of each of the two jambs of the false door is depicted a small unclothed male figure, standing beneath the kilt of the tomb owner and holding his staff. Both bear the name *Ptḥ-špss*, but the one on the left jamb is labelled *zꜣ.f smsw* 'his eldest son' and the slightly smaller figure on the right jamb is *zꜣ.f* 'his son'. As there is a difference in size as well as in designation, it may be possible that two different sons are represented.[29] In the fowling scene on the east wall, at least one of the two males shown in the papyrus skiff with *Jrw-kꜣ-Ptḥ* and his wife may be a son.[30]

II DATING OF IRUKAPTAH

Dates suggested for *Jrw-kꜣ-Ptḥ* range broadly between Dynasty 5 and the First Intermediate Period. Altenmüller has placed him in Dynasty 5 prior to Unis and perhaps as early as Sahure,[31] while the reigns of Neferirkare-Neuserre are preferred by Cherpion,[32] and that of Djedkare by Strudwick.[33] Wiebach also suggests late Dynasty 5,[34] but Dynasty 6 is proposed by both Fischer and Harpur,[35] and late Dynasty 6 to the First Intermediate Period by James and Mekhitarian.[36]

The tomb of *Jrw-kꜣ-Ptḥ* is towards the western end of a number of rock tombs cut on an E-W alignment in the lower part of the southern slope of a natural depression which was subsequently buried during the construction of the Unis

---

28 Ranke, *Personennamen* 1, 326:19.

29 It has generally been assumed that both figures are eldest sons (de Rachewiltz, *Irw-k3-Ptḥ*, 25-26; James, *JEA* 47 [1961], 166; Fischer, *JAOS* 82 [1962], 76).

30 Harpur concludes that in spear fishing and fowling scenes figures standing on the boat in front of, and with their backs to, the tomb owner are family members (*Decoration*, 141, 226).

31 *Chron. d'Ég.* 20 [1945], 80; *Actes XXIXe Congrès* 1, 1-5.

32 *Critères de datation*, 114, 123, 128 (Tables 1, 9, 12).

33 *Administration*, 13.

34 *Scheintür*, 222.

35 Respectively, *JAOS* 82 [1962], 75; *Decoration*, 273. Porter and Moss give early Dynasty 5 or Dynasty 6 (*PM* 3, 639).

36 Respectively, *JEA* 47 [1961], 165; *Painting*, 12.

causeway. The location of his tomb on the southern side of the causeway close to the base of the supporting buttress wall is a compelling argument that it was completed prior to the reign of Unis. Several rock tombs in the eastern part of the area which have been cleared and fully published are dated between the reigns of Neuserre, or perhaps just prior, and early Unis,[37] the construction of the causeway providing a *terminus ante quem.*

Like virtually all of this group, *Jrw-kꜣ-Ptḥ*'s tomb fits Reisner's type RC iva, a N-S corridor chapel with the entrance in the north, a kind of tomb documented only during Dynasties 5 and 6.[38] One of the smallest tombs south of the causeway and, dated early in the reign of Neuserre,[39] possibly the earliest of those decorated, is that of *Nfr* and *Kꜣ.j-ḥꜣ.j*. The largest by far and the one with different architectural features is that of *Nj-ꜥnḫ-H̱nmw* and *H̱nmw-ḥtp*. These two tombs are in the eastern section, with *Nfr*'s cut somewhat west of and at a slightly higher level than that of *Nj-ꜥnḫ-H̱nmw* and *H̱nmw-ḥtp*. The size of the latter is a result of the addition to the original small rock-cut tomb of a large court, two chambers and a pillared portico constructed in stone. The tomb of *Nj-ꜥnḫ-H̱nmw* and *H̱nmw-ḥtp* was enlarged in several stages,[40] like that of *Ptḥ-špss* at Abusir in which they are depicted.[41] It is likely that both tombs were begun late in the reign of Neuserre, and expanded and completed perhaps early in Djedkare's reign.[42]

Of the other tombs south of the causeway that of *Jrw-kꜣ-Ptḥ*, in the western group, appears to be one of the largest and differs from them all in that it has a large number of engaged statues. Rock-cut statuary is documented in only two other tombs at Saqqara,[43] both with a probable date in the latter part of Dynasty 5. Stylistically *Jrw-kꜣ-Ptḥ*'s statues, with a rigid stance and wearing a moustache and a kilt with hanging strands of beads, may be compared to those in the round dated from mid-Dynasty 5 to the beginning of Dynasty 6.[44]

The false door of *Jrw-kꜣ-Ptḥ* is of the type with a cavetto cornice and torus moulding which appeared at Saqqara early in Dynasty 5 but is not commonly attested before the reign of Neuserre.[45] Cavetto cornice doors with torus moulding and two jambs are also found in the two tombs, in the eastern group, which are decorated in paint on plaster rather than in relief, belonging to *Jrj.n-kꜣ-Ptḥ* and to

---

37 Moussa - Altenmüller, *Nefer*, 18; idem, *Nianchchnum*, 44-45; Moussa - Junge, *Two Craftsmen*, 18, 35.

38 Reisner, *Giza*, 241, 246, 304.

39 Moussa - Altenmüller, *Nefer*, 18; Cherpion, *Mastabas et hypogées*; 134-35; Harpur, *Decoration*, 189, 276.

40 Moussa - Altenmüller, *Nianchchnum*, 14-16.

41 Verner, *Ptahshepses*, photo 55, pl. 34. For the building stages see the plan in Verner, *Forgotten Pharaohs*, 175.

42 Respectively, Moussa - Altenmüller, *Nianchchnum*, 44-45; Strudwick, *Administration*, 89-90. Tomb enlargement, usually corresponding with a significant increase in wealth at the beginning of a reign after some disruption, is evident in tombs of higher officials early in the reigns of Neuserre, Djedkare and Unis (Kanawati, *Egyptian Administration*, 77, graphs I-II).

43 Mariette, *Mastabas*, 403; Emery, *JEA* 51 [1965], 6, pl. 2:2.

44 For discussion and comparisons see below under "Statues".

45 Rusch, *ZÄS* 58 [1923], 113; Reisner, *Giza*, 378-79; Vandier, *Manuel* 2, 401-403; Wiebach, *Scheintür*, 133-35; Strudwick, *Administration*, 13-15, 35.

Sḫntjw and *Nfr-sšm-Ptḥ*.[46] The similar door in the tomb of *Jrw-kꜣ-Ptḥ*, in the western group, has, perhaps uniquely, only a single jamb which may suggest a transitional and earlier attempt. His neighbour to the west, *3ḫt-ḥtp*, has a flat framed door with an offering list on the panel and jamb,[47] a type attested at Saqqara from Neferirkare to Djedkare.[48] Older style false doors are also found in the eastern group in the tombs of *Nfr* and *Kꜣ.j-ḥꜣ.j*, which has as well a palace façade false door,[49] and of *Nj-ꜥnḫ-Ḫnmw* and *Ḫnmw-ḥtp*,[50] the two rock tombs south of the causeway with walls cased in limestone.

The owners of tombs south of the Unis causeway were not senior officials of the central administration nor related to the king, but held positions within the royal household that suggest direct and personal service to the king. Their titles, such as overseers of manicurists, metal workers and singers in the palace as well as royal butchers, reflect administrative reforms initiated by Neferirkare-Neuserre which opened the bureaucracy to individuals not connected to the royal family.[51] At this time butchery titles like those held by *Jrw-kꜣ-Ptḥ*, *qbḥ nmt* with the addition of *pr-ꜥꜣ* and those formed with *ꜥbw-r nswt*, make their appearance and are attested almost exclusively at Saqqara between the reigns of Neuserre and Pepy I.

In mid-Dynasty 5 there also appear new elements in tomb decoration strongly influenced by artistic developments in the royal temples of the first half of Dynasty 5. Among those particularly relevant to the tomb of *Jrw-kꜣ-Ptḥ* are the use of the cavetto cornice door and scenes of marsh activities.[52] According to Harpur a number of the themes found in *Jrw-kꜣ-Ptḥ*'s tomb were introduced in private tombs in the reign of Neuserre. These include a punter in a fishing or fowling scene,[53] a hippopotamus hunt,[54] shoulder straps worn by haulers in dragnet scenes,[55] and a calf tied to the boat or held by a man in the stern in fording scenes.[56] In addition, the four known double bed-making scenes are all at Saqqara in tombs dated to late Dynasty 5-beginning Dynasty 6.[57]

The motif in *Jrw-kꜣ-Ptḥ*'s tomb of a lotus held to the nose by a male tomb owner in a wall scene is rare and attested in two closely contemporary tombs, *Jj-mrjj* at Giza[58] and *Nj-ꜥnḫ-Ḫnmw* and *Ḫnmw-ḥtp* in the Unis causeway.[59] Both are

46 Moussa - Junge, *Two Craftsmen*, fig. 1, ills. 1-3.
47 Zayed, *ASAE* 55 [1958], pls. 2-5.
48 Strudwick, *Administration*, 28-29; he compares this door stylistically with that of *Ṯjj*.
49 Moussa - Altenmüller, *Nefer*, pls. 28-29, 31-32, 36, 39.
50 Idem, *Nianchchnum*, pls. 81a, 92, fig. 26.
51 Baer, *Rank and Title*, 300; Strudwick, *Administration*, 337-38.
52 For discussion see below "Scenes and Inscriptions." Harpur remarks on the dominance of water themes in *Jrw-kꜣ-Ptḥ*'s tomb (*Decoration*, 190).
53 Ibid, 257, 355-63 (Table 7.26), the first example dated to late Neuserre.
54 Ibid, 261, 335-63 (Table 7.7). An example may occur at the end of Dynasty 4 but others date from Neuserre on with most in the period Djedkare-Pepy I.
55 Ibid, 189, 259, 335-63 (Table 7.73).
56 Ibid, 192, 260, 335-63 (Table 7.93), most attested from Djedkare-early Dynasty 6.
57 *Sḫntjw* and *Nfr-sšm-Ptḥ*, *Jj-nfrt*, *Ptḥ-ḥtp/Jj-n-ꜥnḫ* and *Jrw-kꜣ-Ptḥ*, see below "Scenes and Inscriptions".
58 Weeks, *Cemetery G 6000*, pl. 36.
59 Moussa - Altenmüller, *Nianchchnum*, fig. 20, pl. 50.

known to have enlarged their original tombs. A number of additions were made during the reign of Neuserre to the four-generation family complex of *Jj-mrjj*, who may have died early in the reign of Menkauhor.[60] The scene depicting *Nj-ꜥnḫ-H̱nmw* smelling a lotus is prominently positioned on the impressive decorated entrance vestibule built of stone which leads to the limestone-cased rock-cut chambers of the second building stage. This may have been late in the reign of Neuserre, but certainly prior to the final large addition which may have occurred early in Djedkare's reign. It is highly likely that this theme, so visible on the early entrance to *Nj-ꜥnḫ-H̱nmw*'s tomb, was the inspiration for the artist who decorated the tomb of *Jrw-kꜣ-Ptḥ*.

Many of the themes of *Jrw-kꜣ-Ptḥ*'s wall decoration occur in other tombs at Saqqara, both in the causeway and elsewhere, dated between Neuserre and Djedkare, for example *Ḥtp-ḥr-ꜣḫtj*, *Kꜣ.j-m-rmṯ*, *Ꜣḫt-ḥtp* and in particular *Ṯjj* and *Nj-ꜥnḫ-H̱nmw* and *H̱nmw-ḥtp*. In the tomb of the latter, in addition to the tomb owner smelling a lotus, may be mentioned punters in a fishing and fowling scene and the paired loaves with a single outward facing loaf at each end on the offering table of the false door panel. Other motifs common to both tombs include a hedgehog travelling boat with oars, the tomb owner standing in a boat holding a staff in front of him, a corpulent overseer in the dragnet scene and the haulers wearing shoulder straps, all of which also appear in the tomb of *Ṯjj*. Depicted in the tombs of *Ṯjj* and *Jrw-kꜣ-Ptḥ* are chairs with both bull's and lion's legs, a papyriform boat under sail and an overseer leaning on a staff in the middle of a dragnet scene.[61]

It is highly unlikely that *Jrw-kꜣ-Ptḥ* can be assigned a date prior to mid-Dynasty 5, before *Nfr* and *Kꜣ.j-ḥꜣ.j*. Nor is it certain that the tombs south of the causeway were constructed chronologically from west to east as proposed by Altenmüller.[62] The eastern and western sections each have examples of the older type of false door and the new cavetto cornice door. A number of scenes in *Jrw-kꜣ-Ptḥ*'s tomb may well have been influenced by the finely executed and original wall decoration of the large multi-chambered tomb of *Nj-ꜥnḫ-H̱nmw* and *H̱nmw-ḥtp*. On the basis of *Jrw-kꜣ-Ptḥ*'s titles and motifs in his wall scenes which are not attested prior to Neuserre, the use of a cavetto cornice door which became more common during the reign of that king, as well as the iconography of his engaged statuary, a date no earlier than Neuserre is reasonably certain. *Jrw-kꜣ-Ptḥ*'s tomb was probably begun shortly after the early building stages of *Nj-ꜥnḫ-H̱nmw* and *H̱nmw-ḥtp* at the end of the reign of Neuserre and, like it, is largely decorated in relief; but with a painted and probably unfinished wall scene as well as a cavetto cornice door, it may be more closely contemporary with *Jrj.n-kꜣ-Ptḥ*, *Sḫntjw* and *Nfr-sšm-Ptḥ*. While the relative dating of these tombs is uncertain, they were probably cut and decorated within a very short time of each other in the period prior to the reign of Unis and the construction of his causeway.

Suggested date: Late Dynasty 5, Menkauhor - Djedkare

---

60 *Weeks, Cemetery G 6000,* 4-5.

61 For references and comments see under "Scenes and Inscriptions".

62 *Actes XXIXe Congrès*, 3-4.

III ARCHITECTURAL FEATURES

Pls. 5-7, 38-40

The tomb of *Jrw-kȝ-Ptḥ* is one in a row of eleven rock-cut tombs on the south side of the Unis causeway which were excavated by Abd el-Salam Mohammed Hussein in 1940 and appear on his site map published, following his early death, some years later.[63] Those positioned east of *Jrw-kȝ-Ptḥ* have since been reburied under sand and lie behind the south wall of the modern stairway built parallel to, and just south of, the causeway by the Saqqara Inspectorate of Antiquities. These stairs now provide access to the tombs of *Jrw-kȝ-Ptḥ* and his neighbours to the west, *Nj-ʿnḫ-Rʿ* and *ȝḫt-ḥtp*. They are situated 200.0-210.0m. east of the mortuary temple of Unis, about 10.5m. south of, and over 9.0m. below, the axis of the causeway floor. The three tombs, adjacent to each other in an E-W alignment, face the base of the stepped buttress wall of large, well-shaped but undressed blocks built up from the ground level of a natural depression and overlaid with a compact fill on which the causeway was constructed (floor SP 50.25). The top-cut of the rock cliff behind and to the south of these tombs today rises nearly 17.0m. (SP 57.89) above the court level of *Jrw-kȝ-Ptḥ* (SP 41.02).

Like those of *Nj-ʿnḫ-Rʿ* and *ȝḫt-ḥtp*, the tomb of *Jrw-kȝ-Ptḥ* is partly constructed in masonry and partly rock-cut, and is oriented N-S with the entrance in the north wall. It consists of two rooms, a court built largely of limestone blocks and a corridor chapel cut into the rock slope which corresponds with Reisner's type RC iva.[64] Five burial shafts are cut into the floor of the chapel. There is no evidence of any decoration in the court, but preserved in the offering chapel are brightly painted relief decoration on the north and east walls, a limestone false door and 14 engaged statues. The rock in this area is a limestone conglomerate with bands of shale and thin quartz intrusions and is of sufficient quality to permit relief decoration and the use of rock-cut statuary.

The north, façade wall of the court facing the causeway buttress wall is constructed entirely of well-dressed limestone blocks, the four remaining courses standing to a maximum height of 1.40m. The entrance is defined by a recess .20m. deep which extends .80m. to the west of the doorway and 1.15m. to the east, where the lines have been obscured by the contemporary access stairway. Neither the original width nor height of the façade and its entrance recess can be determined. The doorway measures .55m. wide x .85m. thick and has an internal recess 1.05m. wide x .20m. deep.[65] The doorway opens into a court 3.90m. N-S x 1.75m. E-W at the north wall and 1.60m. at the south wall. While the north wall is totally constructed, the floor and the south wall are hewn into the native rock. The southern end of the east wall is cut into the mountain but as it slopes downward roughly dressed blocks of limestone are bonded with the rock, and the

---

63 Zayed, *ASAE* 55 [1958], pl. 1; de Rachewiltz, *Irw-k3-Ptḥ*, pl. 1. Hussein did not include the mastaba of *Nfr-ḥr-n-Ptḥ*, the so-called 'bird tomb', which was constructed in masonry immediately west of, and at the approximate roof level, of the others.

64 *Giza* 1, 241. The entire group of eleven tombs appear to have the same N-S corridor-type chapel, with some variations (see map of Hussein in de Rachewiltz, *Irw-k3-Ptḥ*, pl. 1).

65 The two steps presently in the entrance are a construction of the Saqqara Inspectorate.

northern part of the wall is constructed of masonry.[66] The opposite west wall, while also cut into the mountain slope, is formed of limestone blocks which case the native rock at the southern end and are freestanding in the northern part where a fill separates it from the east wall of *3ḫt-ḥtp*. The stone blocks of these walls were positioned with the aid of a buff-coloured plaster, not a true mortar. The constructed east and west walls of the court are broken in the northern part and stand to a present height of 1.20m. but the southern parts, cut entirely in rock, are fully preserved to the original height of 2.35m. At the western end of the south wall is a fragment of original plaster, a sandy and coarse pinkish gypsum, but there is no evidence that the court was ever decorated.

A doorway leading to the chapel is cut into the south wall and has the same axis, parallel to the west wall, as the entrance in the north wall of the court. It is surmounted by a lintel .35m. high which projects .075m. and spans the entire wall. The doorway measures .70m. wide x .75m. thick x 2.00m. high, the ceiling sloping slightly downward to produce an internal height of 1.96m. Traces of plaster on both door thicknesses clearly indicate the outlines of a now missing drum, .25m. thick, possibly a separate limestone element. Like the flat-bottom limestone drum preserved in the adjacent tomb of *3ḫt-ḥtp*,[67] it may have been inscribed with the tomb owner's name and titles. Other remnants of plaster are preserved on the west door thickness which retains as well a few traces of faded red paint. Faint remains of red colour are also found on the door thicknesses of *3ḫt-ḥtp*. Presumably the present threshold of the doorway and the step which houses a metal door installed to secure the tomb are not original. De Rachewiltz reported three steps with rises of .13m., .28m. and .14m.[68] Currently, a step of .25m. leads down to a recess 1.05m. wide x .18m. deep on the east side and .30m. on the west, and a second step down of .175m. gives access to the chapel.

The doorway opens into the chapel at the west end of the north wall. The long corridor-type chamber is not cut on the same N-S alignment as the court but angled 5° to the east. The chamber measures 13.55m. N-S at the east wall x 13.35m. at the west wall x 2.25m. E-W at the north wall and 2.15m. at the south wall, with an average height of 2.35m. The ceiling rises to 2.42m. at the NE corner and portions of the ceiling have flaked away in the southern part of the room, between the recess in the west wall and the serdab in the east wall. In addition to measures taken to secure the chapel and to stabilize and preserve its wall decoration and statues, the Department of Restoration at the Saqqara Inspectorate covered the floor with cement tiles ca .10-.14m. thick. All measurements of height are based on the present floor level, which closely approximates the original.[69]

The chapel is quite well-cut in rock of reasonable quality which exhibits a number of faults and fractures. One major fault runs from the kilt of statue 5 on the east

---

66 A rubble fill behind the limestone blocks indicated on the plan of Hussein is now hidden by a retaining wall built perpendicular to the modern stairway.

67 Badawi, *ASAE* 40 [1941], pl. 47. A similar drum also forms part of the constructed stone façade of *Nj-ꜥnḫ-Rꜥ*.

68 *Irw-k3-Ptḥ*, 5. This results in a height from the threshold to the chapel floor of .55m. as against the current measurement of .425m.

69 The sill height given by de Rachewiltz for the statues on the west wall of .45-.46m. (ibid, 27) is virtually identical to that found today.

wall up to the ceiling, progresses diagonally southward and then down the west wall towards the arm of the northernmost statue. Another runs south from the ceiling above the southernmost statue on the west wall to the south wall where it continues down to the floor. Necessary repairs were made at the time of construction with a coarse pinkish plaster with sandy inclusions. The ceiling, south wall and the southern portions of the east and west walls, including the west wall recess, show no evidence of having been smoothed or plastered. The north wall and the east and west walls north of the serdab and recess were roughly smoothed and coated with a thin plaster prior to their decoration, largely in relief.

Cut into the walls are a total of 14 niches which hold individual statues carved in high relief, two in the north wall, eight in the east wall and four in the west wall. Those on the north and east walls have a sill height of .25m. and average .44m. wide x 1.35m. high, and are separated by piers .14m. wide. Those on the west have a sill height of .45m. with dimensions averaging .62m. wide x 1.62m. high, the average width of the piers between them .42m.

An entry cut into the southern part of the east wall at a height of .30m. above the floor measures .65m.(av.) wide x 1.15m. high at the north side and 1.05m. at the south x .30m. thick. It opens into an irregularly cut chamber in the shape of a parallelogram with dimensions averaging 1.65m. N-S x 1.10m. E-W x 1.10m. high. This small chamber was probably a serdab which was, presumably, sealed by a wall of mud brick. At the time de Rachewiltz cleared the tomb a quantity of mud bricks remained on the floor directly in front of this room,[70] and he found in this "annexe" an unfinished limestone statuette of a seated male figure together with some roughly hand-made pottery scattered on the floor.[71] Two metres south of the niche a narrow ledge was left in the rock of the east wall at a height of ca. 1.00m. above the floor. Very roughly shaped, it measures approximately .85m. long x .10m. wide x .15m. thick.

Set into the west wall at its south end is a monolithic limestone false door .76m. wide x 2.20m. high with a cavetto cornice, torus moulding and a single pair of jambs. The measurements of the door are: cavetto cornice .65m. wide x .19m. high, torus moulding .06m. thick, upper lintel .65m. wide x .12m. high, central panel .45m. wide x .40m. high with side apertures each .10m. wide, lower lintel .65m. wide x .14m. high, jambs .25m. wide x 1.10m. high, central niche .15m. wide x .15m. deep x .90m. high, drum .14m. thick. Below the jambs and torus moulding is a base .18m. high. The cornice, side apertures and base are shaped, but not smoothed like the remaining surfaces which are coated with a thin layer of plaster and decorated. A recess cut into the west wall immediately north of the false door measures 1.90m. wide x .55m. deep and is the full height of the chapel. Its purpose is unknown, but it can be noted that there is a similar-sized recess next to the false door in the west wall of the adjacent tomb of *3ḫt-ḥtp*.[72]

---

70 *Irw-k3-Ptḥ*, 5-6, pls. 5-6.

71 Ibid, 29-30, fig. 6, pls. 26:2, 27, 28. Roth comments that as burial chambers decreased in size and held less, serdabs may have assumed some of their functions and held funerary equipment (*Palace Attendants*, 56-57).

72 Badawi, *ASAE* 40 [1941], pl. 47.

Burial Apartments

Five square-mouthed shafts were cut into the floor of the chapel contiguous with the east wall. These shafts were recleared in 1999 in order to obtain measurements to complete the architectural plans and descriptions. De Rachewiltz made no mention of any finds,[73] nor were any encountered in the recent clearing. All five shafts are cleanly cut in the native rock with walls at right angles, but the small burial chambers are rough, unfinished and largely shapeless.

1 Shaft 1 is positioned immediately south of the unfinished statue and .05m. from the east wall. Its mouth measures 1.30m. N-S on the east wall and 1.26 on the west x 1.28m. E-W on the north wall and 1.30m. on the south. Ledges .20-.22m. wide were left along the north and west walls at a depth of .53m. below the chapel floor which reduce the size of the shaft to 1.08m. square. The shaft descends vertically for a further 2.92m. to reach a total depth of 3.45m. The floor of the shaft is 1.05m. square and there is no burial chamber.

2 Cut .67m. south of shaft 1 and .20m. from the east wall, shaft 2 has a mouth 1.05m. square, the walls expanding as they descend to produce measurements at the floor of 1.12m. E-W x 1.15m. N-S on the east wall and 1.20m. on the west wall. The shaft is cut to a maximum depth of 4.70m., the floor sloping sharply downward from east to west. An opening .70m. high across the west wall and a step down of .25m. leads to a small roughly cut burial chamber, its sloping floor and ceiling following the same angle of the shaft floor. It is virtually shapeless with no clean lines and average measurements of 2.20m. N-S x 1.15m. E-W x 1.00m. high.

3 Shaft 3 gives access to the main burial chamber. The mouth, 1.30m. square, is cut .20m. from the east wall and directly in front of the serdab. The shaft descends to a depth of 4.92m., the walls expanding slightly to provide measurements at the floor of 1.32m. N-S on the east wall and 1.38m. on the west x 1.42m. E-W. At the floor of the shaft an opening cut the full width of the west wall x 1.20m. high leads to a burial chamber. After the burial this entry was sealed by a wall .35m. thick x 1.26m. high constructed of flat undressed pieces of limestone and mud bricks, portions of which remain *in situ*. Cut to the west and south to lie beneath the false door, the burial chamber has no clean corners or surfaces and maximum measurements of 3.05m. N-S x 2.25m. E-W x 1.20m. high. Only the eastern part of the north wall and a section of the ceiling inside the entrance about 1.40m. square, are reasonably well-cut. The west and south walls are very rough and unfinished and the ceiling in the southern part slopes unevenly and sharply downward.

4 Lying .57m. south of shaft 3, the mouth of shaft 4 measures 1.06m. N-S x 1.10m. E-W, with the east wall cut .15m. under the east wall of the chapel. The shaft descends to a depth of 5.40m. with a narrow and rough ledge, averaging .10m. wide, left along the east and north walls at a depth of 2.85m. As they descend the east and west walls of the shaft narrow slightly and the north and south walls expand slightly to give measurements at the shaft floor of

---

73 For information recorded by de Rachewiltz see *Irw-k3-Ptḥ*, 29.

1.00m. N-S x 1.12m. E-W on the north wall and 1.27m. at the south wall. An opening .94m. high cut across the width of the east wall at a height of .46m. above the floor gives access to a small burial area cut to the north. It measures 1.50m. N-S on the west wall and 1.57m. on the east wall x 1.00m. E-W with a ceiling sloping from .94m. at the west wall to .61m. at the east wall.

5 Shaft 5 is located in the SE corner of the chapel floor, its mouth undercutting both the south and east walls by .10m. The mouth measures 1.10m. N-S x 1.02m. E-W on the south wall and 1.06m. on the north wall. The shaft has a maximum depth to a floor sloping downward to the west of 4.85m. Cut across the west wall is an opening .80m. high which leads to a very irregularly and roughly cut burial chamber. Its average dimensions are 2.20m. N-S x 1.00m. E-W, the floor following the same slope as the shaft to give a height of 1.00m. at the west wall.

Commentary

Some twenty Old Kingdom rock-cut tombs, many anonymous, are presently known in the area immediately south of the Unis causeway, the majority published in plan with no architectural detail.[74] Nevertheless, based on the available but incomplete information, a few observations may be made. The tombs may be divided geographically into a western group and an eastern group at the base of the causeway, with another in the eastern part which is cut at a slightly higher level.

All but a few of these tombs correspond to Reisner's type RC iva, a N-S corridor chapel with the entrance in the north wall.[75] Most, as far as can be discerned, had a small rectangular open court in front of the entrance, either constructed in stone or brick, rock-cut, or a combination of the two. The one tomb with significant architectural differences is the largest, that of *Nj-ʿnḫ-Ḫnmw* and *Ḫnmw-ḥtp*, which was built in stages.[76] The earlier incorporated a N-S corridor, an E-W offering chamber to the west and a serdab all cut in rock, with an entrance vestibule constructed in stone. To this was subsequently added a large court and, to its east, two chambers with a new entry provided by a pillared portico in the north wall, all built of fine quality limestone blocks. The two rock-hewn chambers of this tomb, most of the chapel of *Nfr* and *Kꜣ.j-ḥꜣ.j* and a section of the west wall of *Jrj.n-kꜣ-Ptḥ* provide the only evidence of stone casing of the rock walls. However, limestone is used on the façade and/or entrance elements in numerous tombs and for all but four of the false doors.

The architectural information is minimal for many tombs, particularly in the western group, but plan outlines suggest that the corridor chapels of the eastern group, with a maximum N-S length of 8.70m., are smaller than those to the west

74 Badawi, *ASAE* 40 [1941], pl. 47; de Rachewiltz, *Irw-k3-Ptḥ*, pl. 1; Moussa - Altenmüller, *Nefer*, fig. 1; idem, *Nianchchnum*, fig. 1; Moussa - Junge, *Two Craftsmen*, fig. 1.

75 Reisner, *Giza*, 241-42. The Giza examples cited by Reisner are, however, smaller than the Unis causeway tombs. Note that the westernmost of the tombs adjacent to the causeway with the entrance on the east rather than the north, that of *Nfr-ḥr-n-Ptḥ*, is not included in this discussion. It is a mastaba fully constructed in stone on top of an earlier rock-cut tomb and therefore later than the others, probably no earlier than late Unis and possibly Teti.

76 Moussa - Altenmüller, *Nianchchnum*, 14-16.

of which *Jrw-kꜣ-Ptḥ*, averaging 13.45m. N-S, appears to be one of the largest. The known heights of the rock-cut chapels range from 1.90m. to 2.35m. while the constructed rooms of *Nj-ꜥnḫ-H̱nmw* and *H̱nmw-ḥtp* have ceilings 3.95m. high.

The entrances, all in the north wall, are generally located west of the corridor axis but are east of the axis in the group of five at a slightly higher level, including that of *Nfr* and *Kꜣ.j-ḥꜣ.j*, which are probably slightly earlier than the others.

Five tombs have serdabs in the south wall, but that of *Nj-ꜥnḫ-H̱nmw* and *H̱nmw-ḥtp* lies to the west of the offering chapel and that of *Jrw-kꜣ-Ptḥ* is cut into the east wall.

All wall decoration in the tomb of *Nj-ꜥnḫ-H̱nmw* and *H̱nmw-ḥtp* and most of *Nfr* and *Kꜣ.j-ḥꜣ.j* is executed in painted relief on a casing of limestone blocks. The north section of the west wall of *Jrj.n-kꜣ-Ptḥ* is lined with stone but the rest of the tomb is coated with mud plaster and decorated in paint as is the neighbouring tomb of *S̱ḫntjw* and *Nfr-sšm-Ptḥ*. *Jrw-kꜣ-Ptḥ* is the sole tomb in the western group known to have painted wall scenes carved in the native rock;[77] a portion of the east wall in paint only is almost certainly unfinished. *Jrw-kꜣ-Ptḥ*'s tomb is also unique among the group in the Unis causeway in its extensive use of rock-cut statuary, being one of three known examples at Saqqara.

The false doors recorded are generally carved in limestone except for the two adjacent tombs in the eastern section decorated in paint on plaster. All three doors in the tomb of *S̱ḫntjw* and *Nfr-sšm-Ptḥ* are cut in the native rock, while in that of *Jrj.n-kꜣ-Ptḥ* one false door is rock-cut and the other, unfinished, cut into the limestone wall casing.[78] Three of these five doors are of the type with cavetto cornice, torus moulding and two jambs.[79] The older style of door with a single pair of jambs enclosed within a flat frame[80] is found in the tombs of *Nfr* and *Kꜣ.j-ḥꜣ.j*, *Nj-ꜥnḫ-H̱nmw* and *H̱nmw-ḥtp* in the eastern groups and of *ꜣḫt-ḥtp*, which includes an offering list on the panel and jambs,[81] in the western. The false doors of *Nfr* and *Kꜣ.j-ḥꜣ.j*, possibly the earliest of the tombs, are cut into the limestone casing; four depict a figure in the central niche and another provides the only example in the causeway area of a palace façade door.[82] The large twin doors of *Nj-ꜥnḫ-H̱nmw* and *H̱nmw-ḥtp* appear to be formed of several large blocks of stone, while their small ones are carved into the wall casing, as are those adjacent of their wives. The door of *ꜣḫt-ḥtp* is a monolithic block set into the rock, as is the sole cavetto cornice false door known in the western group, that of *Jrw-kꜣ-Ptḥ,* which has a single pair of jambs.

Most of the published tombs have at least three shafts, the largest number of eleven found in each of the two which are cased in limestone, *Nfr* and *Kꜣ.j-ḥꜣ.j* and

---

77 In the eastern group scenes in rock-cut relief occur only in the alcove in the east wall of *Nfr* and *Kꜣ.j-ḥꜣ.j* (Moussa - Altenmüller, *Nefer*, 12).

78 Moussa - Junge, *Two Craftsmen*, fig. 1, ills. 1-3.

79 Rusch, *ZÄS* 58 [1963], 120 pl. A: II.2.

80 Ibid, 122 pl. B: I.1. The small unfinished doors of the wives of the two brothers (Moussa - Altenmüller, *Nianchchnum*, pl. 81a) have two jambs and a frame (Rusch, 122 pl. B: III.4).

81 Zayed, *ASAE* 55 [1958], pls. 2-5.

82 Moussa- Altenmüller, *Nefer*, pls. 29, 31-32, 36, 39.

Nj-ˁnḫ-H̱nmw and *H̱nmw-ḥtp*. The vast majority are square vertical shafts, but the main burial chambers of *Sḫntjw*, *Nfr-ssm-Ptḥ*, *Nj-ˁnḫ-H̱nmw* and *H̱nmw-ḥtp* and *3ḫt-ḥtp* are reached by shallow sloping passages, the last two each with a limestone sarcophagus *in situ*. Like *Jrw-kꜣ-Ptḥ*, five shafts are aligned adjacent to the east wall of the N-S corridor chapel in the tombs of *Nj-ˁnḫ-H̱nmw* and *H̱nmw-ḥtp* and of *Sḫntjw* and *Nfr-ssm-Ptḥ*. None of the finished shafts have a depth greater than 5.30m. other than shaft No. 4 of *Jrw-kꜣ-Ptḥ* which is 5.40m.

IV SCENES AND INSCRIPTIONS

Pls. 8, 41

Decoration of the offering chapel in raised relief is limited to the north wall and to a length of 10 metres on the east wall north of the serdab. The scenes are largely confined to the upper part of both walls above a horizontal line of text, except for a narrow panel at the north end of the east wall and registers with boats in the southern part. A full-height panel in the middle of the east wall depicting marsh activities is executed solely in paint. Inscriptions, a few in paint but most incised, are minimal and restricted to the name and titles of the tomb owner, a single line with a standard *ḥtp dj nswt* formula and the false door. No captions or descriptive texts accompany the wall scenes, nor is there an offering list. There is evidence of changes to the decorative program.

North Wall

BED-MAKING AND FURNISHINGS

Pls. 9, 42

The upper part of the narrow north wall east of the entrance doorway, 1.13m. wide, is occupied by scenes of bed-making and furnishings. The theme is repeated in two registers of unequal heights, the upper .32m. high and the lower .22m. at the west end and .24m. at the east. Outlines, detail and colour are poorly preserved, the west end of the upper register retaining no decoration and possibly never finished. In both registers the figures and beds are oriented to the right,[83] towards a seated figure of the tomb owner at the north end of the east wall. The bed and canopy in each register are very similar. As usual, the wooden bed frame with papyrus umbel finials and bull's legs slopes slightly downward from the head to the foot and the mattress also slopes, being thicker at the head of the bed than at the foot. The bed in the upper register appears to lack a footboard, which is shown in the lower register and in virtually all well-preserved Memphite examples.[84]

---

83 Animal legs, bull's or lion's, on beds habitually face the bed-head; an exception is documented in Upper Egypt in Dynasty 6 (Davies, *Deir el-Gebrâwi* 2, pl. 23).

84 Another exception is found in the tomb of *Nbt*, also in the Unis Cemetery (Munro, *Unas-Friedhof*, pl. 22).

Each bed is placed beneath a flat canopy[85] supported by five wooden posts with rounded tops.[86]

All attendants in both registers wear short cap wigs that expose the ear and plain kilts. Two men stand near the bed in the upper register. The first is beside the bed with his arms stretched out, a headrest in his left hand and a fly whisk in his right. Near the foot of the bed, the second man holds in his right hand another fly whisk and in his left a long wooden stick that, although the lines are unclear, appears to turn down at the top and may be a staff.[87] Behind him is a low table,[88] executed in paint and poorly preserved. Five men are depicted in the lower register, two standing beside the bed on which is laid a headrest.[89] The first attendant bends forward over the bed to smooth it and another, directly behind him, extends his arms towards the bed with a fly whisk in his left hand and a headrest[90] in his right. To the left of the bed two men facing each other carry between them a large piece of furniture with bull's legs that is unlikely to be a chest as suggested by de Rachewiltz.[91] It is probably an armchair with a high back portrayed in a frontal aspect, as similarly carried by two men in the transportation of furnishings in the nearby tomb of *3ḫt-ḥtp*, as well as in that of *Ṯjj*.[92] Behind them follows a third

85 As far as can be distinguished, representations of bed canopies in the capital were flat except for an isolated example in the tomb of *Kȝ.j-m-ꜥnḫ* which has only three uprights and a two-sectioned canopy with shrine-like curves (Junker, *Gîza* 4, fig. 10a). Sixth Dynasty scenes in Upper Egypt consistently had a curved canopy. A canopy is lacking in a second bed-making scene in the tomb of *Kȝ.j-m-ꜥnḫ* (ibid, pl. 14) and in the tombs of *Wr-jr.n-Ptḥ* at Saqqara (James, *Hieroglyphic Texts*, pl. 29), *Ḫntj* (Saleh, *Tombs at Thebes*, pl. 13) and possibly *Hnqw/jj...f* (Davies, *Deir el-Gebrâwi* 2, pl. 23) in Upper Egypt.

86 The outlines are not distinct, but the capitals in these scenes are commonly described as resembling a lotus-bud. Most canopies have seven or more supports, but that of *Nbt* has four (Munro, *Unas-Friedhof*, pl. 22) and *Kȝ.j-m-ꜥnḫ* has three (Junker, *Gîza* 4, fig. 10a), as does probably also *Nj-mȝꜥt-Rꜥ* (Roth, *Palace Attendants*, fig. 187).

87 See a staff with the top in the shape of a hand depicted on a bed of *Kȝ.j-m-ꜥnḫ* (Junker, *Gîza* 4, pl. 14). A staff with a curved top occasionally appears with furnishings (Fischer, *MMJ* 13 [1978], 7-8) and is clearly illustrated in the nearby and closely contemporary tombs of *Nj-ꜥnḫ-Ḫnmw* and *Ḫnmw-ḥtp* (Moussa - Altenmüller, *Nianchchnum*, pls. 60-61) and of *3ḫt-ḥtp* (Ziegler, *Akhethetep*, 168; the original site of the Louvre mastaba has recently been located just north of the Unis causeway). For other examples in the second half of Dynasty 5 see Lepsius, *Denkmäler* II, pls. 78b, 104b; Épron - Wild, *Ti* 2, pl. 126; Quibell, *Saqqara* 3, pl. 62; Simpson, *Festschrift Edel*, 499 fig. 3; Weeks, *Cemetery G 6000*, figs. 18, 32; Roth, *Palace Attendants*, fig. 162. For an early Dynasty 6 example see Altenmüller, *Mehu*, pl. 60.

88 For such identification see Brovarski, *Studies Simpson* 1, 146-47, fig. 10.

89 Headrests on beds are usually, as here, laid on their sides, but upright examples appear in the tombs of *Nbt* (Munro, *Unas-Friedhof*, pl. 22) and *Ḫntj* (Saleh, *Tombs at Thebes*, pl. 13).

90 Two headrests in the same bed-making scene are not otherwise attested, but in addition to that placed on the bed a headrest is depicted among furnishings adjacent to the scene in the tomb of *Mr.s-ꜥnḫ* III (Dunham - Simpson, *Mersyankh III*, fig. 8).

91 *Irw-k3-Ptḥ*, 21.

92 Respectively, Ziegler, *Akhethetep*, 96-97, 169; Épron - Wild, *Ti* 1, pl. 17. An armchair is depicted in profile between two attendants in a bed-making scene of *Kȝ.j-m-ꜥnḫ* (Junker, *Gîza* 4, fig. 10A) and carried in the transport of furnishings in the tomb of *Ptḥ-špss* at Abusir (Verner, *Ptahshepses*, photo 19, pls. 9-10). Armchairs sometimes appear adjacent to bed-making scenes (Dunham - Simpson, *Mersyankh III*, fig. 8; James, *Hieroglyphic Texts*, pl. 29), occasionally with the tomb owner seated (Borchardt, *Denkmäler* 2, 199, pl. 106; Roth,

man, his left hand at his side holding a jar hanging from a rope and his right arm bent across his chest, the hand grasping a bag of linen slung over his left shoulder.[93]

Colour

Male flesh red; hair and eye details black; kilts white. Bed frames and canopy supports, headrests and flail handles in both registers, as well as the staff and armchair are of same type of wood, painted yellow and black. Canopies, beds and footboard cover white outlined in red. Low table in the upper register red. Trace of white preserved on the bag of linen.

Commentary

The attendants are not all the same size and seem to have been drawn to fit the height of whatever space they occupied.[94] In the top register the man beside the bed, drawn to avoid an overlap of his head and the canopy, is shorter than the man behind him. Both beds are the same size but the narrower bottom register has resulted in a noticeable reduction in the height of the canopy, so that the headrest placed on the bed touches the canopy, and the adjacent armchair has the same height as the bed canopy. The three attendants at the left and the one bending over the bed are similar in size, but the figure standing next to the bed is, again, much shorter to fit under the canopy.

Beds are shown in carpentry workshops and occasional other scenes in the Old Kingdom, but bed-making is not a common theme. First attested at Giza towards the end of Dynasty 4 in the rock-cut tombs of Queen *Mr.s-ꜥnḫ* III and her son *Nb-m-ꜣḫtj*,[95] at least another dozen bed-making scenes dating from early Dynasty 5 to early Dynasty 6 are known in the capital cemeteries. The examples are almost evenly divided between tombs belonging to queens and viziers on the one hand, and to lesser officials on the other, and of them nine occur at Saqqara with six of these found in the Unis Cemetery.[96]

Palace Attendants, fig. 187). While attested in Dynasty 4, armchairs are most frequently found in tombs of Dynasty 5 (Cherpion, *Mastabas et hypogées*, 31-32, 154: Criterion 7).

93 Linen bags are often shown in connection with bed-making scenes. Each of seven attendants standing in a row beneath a large bed in the tomb of *Mrrw-kꜣ.j* is labelled *jmj-r sšr* (Duell, *Mereruka*, pls. 92-93).

94 No other bed-making scene in the capital cemeteries shows such a variation in size which is, however, encountered in a Sixth Dynasty example in Upper Egypt (Davies, *Deir el-Gebrâwi* 2, pl. 23).

95 Respectively, Dunham - Simpson, *Mersyankh III*, fig. 8; Hassan, *Gîza* 4, fig. 81. See Harpur, *Decoration*, 81.

96 These numbers include one scene from Dahshur. A convenient list of Old Kingdom examples is provided by Altenmüller, *Studies Simpson* 1, 28 n.3, to which may be added Saad, *ASAE* 40 [1941], 686-87 (*Jj-nfrt*); Reisner, *Giza*, 351-52 (*ꜥnḫ-m-ꜥ-Rꜥ*); James, *Hieroglyphic Texts*, pl. 29 (*Wr-jr.n-Ptḥ*); Roth, *Palace Attendants*, fig. 187 (*Nj-mꜣꜥt-Rꜥ*). It is to be noted that a bed under a canopy is depicted in the burial chamber of the vizier *Nj-ꜥnḫ-bꜣ* at Saqqara (Hassan, *Saqqara* 3, 47, pl. 28B) and another, without a canopy, in that of *Kꜣ.j-m-ꜥnḫ* at Giza (Junker, *Gîza* 4, pl. 14); beds are reported in other burial chambers at Heliopolis (Daressy, *ASAE* 16 [1916], 196, 202). In Dynasty 6 bed-making scenes are

The placement of the bed-making scene high on the entrance wall, over or near the door, first occurs in the tomb of prince *Nb-m-3ḫtj* at Giza.[97] In Dynasty 5 this seems to have been a favoured position in single chamber tombs at Saqqara such as *Jrw-k3-Ptḥ* and including *Wr-jr.n-Ptḥ*, *Sḫntjw* and *Nfr-sšm-Ptḥ*, and *Ptḥ-ḥtp/Jj-n-ꜥnḫ*.[98] Headrests, flails, clothing and furniture,[99] as well as attendants, are commonly depicted in, or accompanying, bed-making scenes. Neither of the scenes in the tomb of *Jrw-k3-Ptḥ*, nor any of the examples at Giza, show an attendant kneeling on the bed, a motif which appears towards the end of Dynasty 5 at Saqqara. There it is documented in the tombs of *Sḫntjw* and *Nfr-sšm-Ptḥ*, *Nbt*, *Jj-nfrt* and *Ptḥ-ḥtp/Jj-n-ꜥnḫ*,[100] as well as those of *Mḥw* and *Mrrw-k3.j* early in Dynasty 6.[101] At about same time, also at Saqqara, lion's legs appear on beds in scenes in the tombs of the viziers *Mḥw*, *Nj-ꜥnḫ-b3* and *Mrrw-k3.j*.[102] As far as can be determined, in addition to that of *Jrw-k3-Ptḥ*, double images of the bed-making scene in the Memphite cemeteries are limited to three tombs at Saqqara dated from the latter part of Dynasty 5 to the beginning of Dynasty 6:[103] *Sḫntjw* and *Nfr-sšm-Ptḥ*[104] and the vizier *Jj-nfrt*[105] in the Unis Cemetery, and *Ptḥ-ḥtp/Jj-n-ꜥnḫ*.[106]

East Wall

NORTH END, LOWER PART: OFFERING BEARERS

Pls. 10, 44

A narrow panel .30-.33m. wide in the lower part of the east wall between statue 8 and the north wall is decorated with scenes divided into four registers. From the top, the average height of the registers is .275m., .300m., .265m. and .265m. Depicted in the top register are two butchers who wear an abbreviated kilt tied at the

---

recorded in tombs of five senior officials in Upper Egypt (add to Altenmüller's list Kanawati, *El-Hawawish* 2, fig. 19). See also Vandier, *Manuel* 4, 187-93.

97 Hassan, *Gîza* 4, 140, fig. 81.

98 Respectively, James, *Hieroglyphic Texts*, pl. 29; Moussa - Junge, *Two Craftsmen*, pls. 1-2; Hassan, *Saqqara* 2, 97-98, figs. 39-40, pl. 79. The scene is above the entrance to the offering chamber in the multi-roomed tomb of *Jj-nfrt* (Saad, *ASAE* 40 [1941], 687; personal examination). For a discussion of the connection of Old Kingdom bed-making scenes with the later 'Geburtsschrein', see Altenmüller, *Studies Simpson* 1, 27-37.

99 Brovarski has recently published a commentary on many such items as represented in inventory offering lists (*Studies Simpson* 1, 117-55).

100 Respectively, Moussa - Altenmüller, *Two Craftsmen*, pl. 2; Munro, *Unas-Friedhof*, pl. 22; on site observation; Hassan, *Saqqara* 2, figs. 39, 40.

101 Altenmüller, *Mehu*, pls. 52-53; Duell, *Mereruka*, pls. 93, 141. An attendant kneeling on the bed is also preserved in a scene from the tomb of *Snfrw-jn-jšt.f* at Dahshur (Borchardt, *Denkmäler* 2, 199, pl. 106).

102 Respectively, Altenmüller, *Mehu*, pls. 52-53; Hassan, *Saqqara* 3, pl. 28B; Duell, *Mereruka*, pls. 93, 95. Most Upper Egyptian examples, which date from early Dynasty 6, have lion's legs.

103 In mid-Dynasty 6 at Thebes in the tomb of *Ḫntj* a bed is represented in each of three registers of funerary furnishings; two have curved canopies and the third, with an attendant kneeling on the bed, has none (Saleh, *Tombs at Thebes*, pl. 13).

104 Moussa - Junge, *Two Craftsmen*, pls. 1-2.

105 Saad, *ASAE* 40 [1941], 686-87; on site observation.

106 Hassan, *Saqqara* 2, figs. 39-40, pl. 79.

back and are slaughtering an ox. Based on the other butchery scene in this tomb, the man standing at the left probably wields the knife while the man on the right, kneeling on the neck and chest of the animal, holds the foreleg with both hands. Little remains of the ox, but the ear, eye and horns of the animal are distinct.

Each of the three lower registers depicts two offering bearers oriented towards the engaged statues to the right. All wear short wigs covering the ears and plain kilts. In the second register the first man uses his left hand to balance a ewer and basin on his left shoulder and his right hand, hanging by his side, holds a rope attached to the neck of a small jar. The offering bearer behind him holds in his right hand a similar jar while his left hand supports on his shoulder a tray with a stand on which are placed four loaves. The first man in the third register holds in front of his face a censer with the incense grains clearly depicted, grasping the base in his left hand and lifting the lid with the thumb and forefinger of his right. The position of the right arm, bent at the elbow and twisted high over his head, is both awkward and unusual.[107] The second man in the same register holds in front of him in each hand a length of folded cloth. In the bottom register two offering bearers carry between them a tray on a tall stand, the head of the first man turned back towards the tray which holds two large loaves, a bunch of grapes and a trussed duck.

Colour

A portion of the grey background remains but the scenes are incompletely preserved and retain little colour. Male flesh red; hair and eye details black; kilts white. Register 1: Black eye and yellow horn preserved on the ox. Register 2: Ewer and basin yellow; tray and stand blue holding yellow loaves with light brown shading and white loaves with red detail; jars on rope blue, one with black spots. Register 3: Censer base and cover blue, incense red with black outline. Register 4: Centre loaf yellow with light brown shading; grapes blue with black outline.

Commentary

As a purification ritual prior to the presentation of offerings,[108] censing before a standing or seated figure of a tomb owner, sometimes with his wife, is not uncommon.[109] Censing is also regularly depicted in association with the transport of statues of the tomb owner as found, for example, in the nearby tombs of *3ḫt-ḥtp*, *Nj-ꜥnḫ-Ḫnmw* and *Ḫnmw-ḥtp*, *Jj-nfrt* and *Jdwt*,[110] and elsewhere at Saqqara

---

107 The most comparable representation is in the Saqqara tomb of *Kꜣ.j-gm-n.j* (von Bissing, *Gem-ni-kai* 1, pl. 6). A censer is held high above the attendant's head before each of two statues of *Rꜥ-špss*, but the arm is not twisted (Lepsius, *Denkmäler* II, pl. 64bis).

108 Eaton-Krauss, *Statuary*, 68-69. A scene of censing in the tomb of *Sḫm-kꜣ.j* at Giza is labelled 'fumigating for the ka' (Simpson, *Western Cemetery*, 5, fig. 3).

109 For example Junker, *Gîza* 3, figs. 21, 46; Simpson, *Kawab*, fig. 33; idem, *Western Cemetery*, figs. 3, 41, 43; Moussa - Altenmüller, *Nefer*, pl. 26; Lloyd et al., *Saqqâra Tombs* 2, pl. 22; Altenmüller, *Mehu*, pls. 52-53, 55.

110 Respectively, Ziegler, *Akhethetep*, 106, 108; Moussa - Altenmüller, *Nianchchnum*, pls. 16-17; personal observation; Macramallah, *Idout*, pl. 9A,B. Interestingly, one of the two statues of *Jdwt* is shown holding a lotus to her face, as does *Jrw-kꜣ-Ptḥ* seated in the scene directly above this panel.

in the second half of Dynasty 5.[111] In this panel the scene of censing is so positioned to appear as being performed before an actual statue of *Jrw-kꜣ-Ptḥ*.

NORTH END, UPPER PART: SEATED TOMB OWNER AND OFFERINGS

Pls. 1a, 11-12, 43-44

At the top of the east wall above the four registers just described is a seated figure of the tomb owner who faces, not an offering table, but items of food and drink piled in two registers. The width of the scene is 1.51m. and the total height .54m. at the north end and .52m. at the south.

Jrw-kꜣ-Ptḥ is seated on a chair, the front leg not represented,[112] a bull's leg at the back which unusually lacks a socle,[113] a full rounded cushion with no visible back,[114] and a large papyrus umbel finial. He wears a shoulder length wig, moustache,[115] beard, broad collar and a stiff pointed kilt. His right hand rests on his lap holding a folded cloth and his left hand grasps the stem of a lotus flower held to his face. An inscription painted in front of his face reads: *qbḥ nmt pr-ꜥꜣ Jrw-kꜣ-Ptḥ* 'the libationer and butcher of the palace, Irukaptah'.

In front of *Jrw-kꜣ-Ptḥ* the register is divided into two, the smaller upper sub-register .23m. in height and the lower one .31m., filled with food items. The arrangement of offerings forms a well-balanced composition with three groups in each register. None of the low tables or the trays on stands are exactly the same, being distinguished by slight differences in dimension or shape. The tables and basket on a stand in the upper, narrower register are almost equal in height but shorter than those, also of equal height, which fill the larger, lower register. A carinated stone bowl placed on an independent baseline directly in front of *Jrw-kꜣ-*

---

111 E.g., Lepsius, *Denkmäler* II, pl. 64bis; Épron - Wild, *Ti* 1, pls. 54-55; van de Walle, *Neferirtenef*, pls. 14-15; Mohr, *Hetep-her-akhti*, figs. 3, 6-7.

112 Cherpion concludes that no visible front chair legs, found throughout the Old Kingdom, cannot be used as a criterion for dating (*Mastabas et hypogées*, 41). Chairs with no front legs depicted are attested in the second half of Dynasty 5 at Saqqara in the nearby tombs of *ꜣḫt-ḥtp* (Zayed, *ASAE* 55 [1958], pl. 3), *Nj-ꜥnḫ-Ḫnmw* and *Ḫnmw-ḥtp* (Moussa - Altenmüller, *Nianchchnum*, fig. 25, pl. 69) and *Sḫntjw* and *Nfr-sšm-Ptḥ* (Moussa - Junge, *Two Craftsmen*, ills. 1-2), as well as *Ptḥ-ḥtp/Jj-n-ꜥnḫ* (Hassan, *Saqqara* 2, fig. 34b) and *Kꜣ.j-m-snw* (Firth - Gunn, *Teti Pyr. Cem.* 2, pl. 62).

113 Not included in Cherpion's criteria and rarely attested, other chair legs with no socle are found in Lepsius, *Denkmäler* II, pl. 11; Paget - Pirie, *Ptah-hetep*, pl. 39; Junker, *Gîza* 6, fig. 69, pl. 17A; vol. 8, fig. 6, pl. 5A; Reisner, *Giza*, fig. 257; Badawy, *Iteti*, pls. 10-11.

114 Most of the few representations of this type of cushion in tombs with cartouches are found at Saqqara with the name of Neuserre (Cherpion, *Mastabas et hypogées*, 30, 151: Criterion 5). For examples in the second half of Dynasty 5 see Petrie - Murray, *Memphite Chapels*, pls. 10, 13; Épron - Wild, *Ti* 1, pls. 39, 44; van de Walle, *Neferirtenef*, pls. 1-3; Firth - Gunn, *Teti Pyr. Cem.* 2, pl. 62; Moussa - Altenmüller, *Nefer*, pls. 29, 39; idem, *Nianchchnum*, pls. 28, 87-88; Roth, *Palace Attendants*, fig. 178.

115 While not commonly documented in wall scenes, a tomb owner with a moustache is preserved in tombs of Dynasties 3 and 4 (e.g., Quibell, *Hesy*, pls. 29-32 = CG 1426-1430; Murray, *Saqqara* 1, pl. 1; Fazzini, *Images for Eternity*, 28), and also known in the period mid-Dynasty 5-early Dynasty 6 at Saqqara (Moussa - Altenmüller, *Nianchchnum*, pl. 73; Myśliwiec, *Nowe oblicza Sakkary*, figs 33, 47).

Ptḥ's knee matches the three bowls on a table at the opposite end of the register and was probably added in order to balance the length of the lower register, which extends beyond the upper one at the south end. The jars and loaves on stands are grouped at opposite ends in each register, with trays of fruit and vegetables in the centre of each. Note that the ewers and basins, usually near or under an offering table, are positioned close to the tomb owner at his eye level.

At the left in the upper sub-register is a low wooden table on which are placed three basins with spouted ewers, each painted a different colour presumably to represent different materials, and beneath the table are a carinated wide-mouthed, spouted jar and a beer jug. Adjacent is a curved basket on a low woven stand that holds four loaves, onions, lettuce and what may be a marrow or melon.[116] Under the tray are three loaves and another marrow. At the end of this register is a low wooden table holding several loaves of bread and a bunch of grapes, with a lettuce placed beneath.

On a separate baseline by *Jrw-kꜣ-Ptḥ*'s knee is a carinated stone bowl with a cover secured and tied at the top which is adjacent to the first item in the larger lower register, a basketry tray resting on a tall wicker stand which holds four large loaves and a marrow. To one side of the stand are a loaf and another marrow, and to the other a bag of onions and a calf's head. The centre of this register is occupied by a boat-shaped basket[117] placed on a table with an upturned rim which is supported on a tall stand. The basket is artistically filled with a few loaves, grapes, and figs between two piles of pomegranates,[118] one of which is neatly arranged on an individual woven tray resting on three small containers. Two elongated loaves are laid horizontally on the table on either side of the basket, and beneath the table are four loaves and two marrows. At the south end a wooden table holds three stone bowls, two carinated, with elaborate covers. Between the bowls are two lotus flowers on upright stems, and draped over the cover of the container at the left is a bunch of grapes.

Colour

Seated tomb owner: Chair black and yellow with white cushion. Flesh brown-red; hair, eye details, moustache and beard black. Kilt white; collar traces of cobalt blue. Cloth held white; lotus held red stem and traces of blue on flower.
Inscription: Paint only, blue with black outline.
Offerings: Three low tables of wood yellow and black; three large woven trays white with orange-red detail and outline; large tray and stand, probably of pottery, red. Conical loaves yellow with mid-brown shading at top; elongated loaves placed horizontally yellow with white patches and occasional mid-brown shading; rectangular and hexagonal (under centre tray both registers) loaves white with red detail; all loaves red outline. Lettuces light green; marrows light aqua green (all in

---

116 The identification of this item frequently appearing among piled food offerings is still uncertain, see Wilson, *Food and Drink*, 24; Wilkinson, *Garden*, 59, 105; Darby et al., *Food*, 693; Brewer et al., *Plants and Animals*, 65-66, figs. 6.1, 6.2.

117 See e.g., Paget - Pirie, *Ptah-hetep*, pl. 38; Murray, *Saqqara* 1, pls. 22-23; Simpson, *Western Cemetery*, pl. 32; Verner, *Ptahshepses*, photo 115, pl. 60.

118 The identification of these two fruits is not certain and suggested on the bases of differences in size, shape and colouring.

paint with no outline); onions white with red detail; grapes blue with black detail (paint only top register). Upper register: three ewers and basins on same table blue, yellow and red, each with a white spout;[119] beneath a low carinated bowl red with white spout and red beer jar. Three small containers on woven tray red. Lower register, from left: Carinated stone container and stand mottled blue and black, cover yellow. Centre loaf on tray at left yellow with mid-brown shading on bottom as well as top. Three small containers in boat-shaped basket red, figs yellow with brown shading and outline, pomegranates yellow with clear orange-red detail and outline. Three stone containers (two carinated) on table at right mottled blue and black, lashing black on white, covers yellow with ties green, all outlines black. Lotus stems red, petals blue, bands at top yellow. Calf's head white with black spots and eye, red nostril, outlined in black except for thick red line along neck (where severed?).

Commentary

The stiff pointed kilt of *Jrw-kȝ-Ptḥ* is a correction to the original relief showing a plain kilt and, to make room for its triangular projection, it was also necessary to change the position of the hand by shortening the arm. The new hand that holds a folded cloth and both points of the kilt are in paint only. Ewers and basins placed on the low table in front of the tomb owner also show corrections. The carved outlines of the two original vessels extend beyond the final painted areas, their size reduced in order to paint between them a third ewer and basin.

The rare motif of a male tomb owner smelling a lotus, always shown seated, is attested in the late Old Kingdom on eight false doors but in only three wall scenes.[120] In addition to *Jrw-kȝ-Ptḥ* the scene appears in the tombs of *Jj-mrjj* at Giza[121] and of *Nj-ʿnḫ-H̱nmw* and *H̱nmw-ḥtp* in the Unis Cemetery,[122] both with a probable date no earlier than late in the reign of Neuserre. *Jrw-kȝ-Ptḥ* and *H̱nmw-ḥtp* wear shoulder-length wigs and beards while *Jj-mrjj* wears a short wig, and all three wear a stiff pointed kilt. Unlike *Jrw-kȝ-Ptḥ*, the other two are seated in armchairs, *Jj-mrjj* in a lotus-column pavilion in front of piled offerings and *H̱nmw-ḥtp* before an offering table with offerings piled above. *Jj-mrjj* holds in his other hand a fly whisk while *H̱nmw-ḥtp* extends an empty hand towards the offering table. The stem of the lotus is looped in the hands of *Jj-mrjj* and *H̱nmw-ḥtp* but not in that of *Jrw-kȝ-Ptḥ*. The first two are elsewhere in their tombs similarly depicted a second time seated and holding a lotus, but not to the nose.[123] It is curious that the brother of *H̱nmw-ḥtp*, *Nj-ʿnḫ-H̱nmw*, is nowhere in their joint tomb depicted either holding or smelling a lotus.

---

119 Inscribed ewers depicted on a low table in the tomb of *Ṯjj* are painted yellow and have white spouts (Mariette, *Mastabas*, 237-38).

120 Harpur, *Decoration*, 134-35, 331-32: Table 6.11; to which add Kanawati, *El-Hawawish* 6, fig. 9. Half the false doors with this theme are from Saqqara, with two examples from Giza, one from Dahshur, one from Akhmim and one from Edfu. Women, seated or standing, are frequently shown smelling a lotus, either as a wife, mother or daughter or as tomb owner in their own right.

121 Weeks, *Cemetery G 6000*, fig. 36, pl. 19a.

122 Moussa - Altenmüller, *Nianchchnum*, fig. 20, pl. 50.

123 Weeks, *Cemetery G 6000*, fig. 43; Moussa - Altenmüller, *Nianchchnum*, fig. 25, pl. 69.

NORTH, UPPER PART: BUTCHERY AND OFFERING BEARERS

Pls. 1b, 13-14, 44-45

The south end of the two registers of offerings is punctuated by a tall jar on a high jar-stand which separates that scene from one depicting butchery and a procession of offering bearers. It occupies a length of 3.75m. and has a height of .51m. The butchery scene,[124] consisting of twelve men engaged in the slaughter of four oxen, appears to proceed from south to north and is followed by four men bearing cuts of meat towards the seated figure of *Jrw-kꜣ-Ptḥ*. Three of the oxen are bound in the traditional manner of three legs tied together, leaving one foreleg free, but the fourth, its foreleg already severed, is not bound. The butchers wear short wigs exposing the ears and abbreviated kilts, open in the front and exposing the genitals, with belts tied in a loop at the back. The four butchers working on the first two animals have whetstones[125] tucked into the back of their belts, the first clearly showing one end of a cord attached to the whetstone and the other to the edge of his kilt. Standing in the centre, with two oxen on either side, is a butcher facing right who is using the whetstone, similarly attached to the belt and kilt, to sharpen his knife.[126] This man, unlike the other butchers but like three of the men carrying cuts of meat, wears a wig that covers the ear; possibly he acted as a supervisor.

Each of the three butchers working on a bound ox stands at the rear of the animal facing left and leans forward to cut the foreleg with a knife held in the left hand while the open palm of his right hand presses against the raised foreleg. The knife is usually held in the right hand to sever a foreleg, whether the butcher faces left or right,[127] but isolated examples are known of a knife held in the left hand.[128] The butcher in each operation is assisted by a second butcher standing near the head of the ox, his arms stretched out in front of him to pull back on the upright foreleg with both hands. The active involvement of these six butchers is further indicated by their stance, the legs wide apart, the heels raised with weight on the toes, and one foot of each apparently stepping or pressing on the animal.[129] Kneeling beside each of the two middle oxen and facing the butcher wielding the knife is a smaller male figure wearing a regular kilt. He holds in front of his face with both hands a wide-mouthed jar to catch the blood fresh from the cut.[130] The fourth ox, at the

---

124 For a study of Old Kingdom butchery scenes see Vandier, *Manuel* 5, 128-85.

125 *LÄ* 6, cols. 1240-43.

126 Vandier comments that when sharpening a knife the butcher is usually shown facing right, feet flat on the ground, holding the knife in the right hand and the whetstone in the left (*Manuel* 5, 139), as in this scene.

127 Ibid, 158. For example, Murray, *Saqqara* 1, pl. 7; Épron - Wild, *Ti* 1, pl. 50; Duell, *Mereruka*, pl. 54; El-Khouli - Kanawati, *El-Hammamiya*, pl. 47; Verner, *Ptahshepses*, pls. 12, 19; Weeks, *Cemetery G 6000*, fig. 35.

128 Murray, *Saqqara* 1, pl. 23; von Bissing, *Gem-ni-kai* 2, pl. 26; James, *Khentika,* pls. 22, 32; and if the arms are correctly drawn Badawy, *Nyhetep-Ptah*, fig. 7.

129 This is the only example of butchers on their toes noted by Vandier (*Manuel* 5, 160), but compare Lepsius, *Denkmäler* II, pls. 66-68.

130 See Moussa - Altenmüller, *Nianchchnum*, pl. 86; Hassan, *Gîza* 3, fig. 144. Elsewhere the kneeling figure, sometimes with a variant posture, holds the bowl on the ground (Lepsius, *Ergänzungsband*, pls. 35, 42; Murray, *Saqqara* 1, pl. 23; Simpson, *Sekhem-ankh-Ptah*,

left, has already had its foreleg severed and the binding removed from the other three, with the rear legs now held by a standing man in the crook of his right arm. The animal is being skinned by the only butcher depicted holding his knife in the right hand. Bending over behind him is another butcher who cuts into the entrails with the knife in his left hand while pulling the skin back with the right hand, the ribs clearly visible. The three butchers working on this animal are shown with their feet flat on the ground, like the stationary central figure sharpening a knife.

Adjacent to the last group of butchers are four men bearing cuts of meat, three proceeding north towards the tomb owner seated on the other side of the offerings, and the fourth facing south towards the butchery scene behind them.[131] All wear plain straight kilts and three wear short wigs covering the ears. The offering bearer at the head of the group holds horizontally in both hands the foreleg of an ox. The second also carries a foreleg, but held upright, in his right hand and a trussed duck on a stick in his left. The third man grasps in each hand cords which are tied to cuts of meat, ribs in the right hand and a thigh with the bone in the left. The last man faces the butchers directly behind him who presumably provided the cuts carried by the offering bearers. He holds a foreleg over his left shoulder and a filet in his right hand and, like the butchers, wears a wig that exposes the ear.

Colour

The butchers and offering bearers follow traditional conventions with brown-red flesh, black hair and eyes, white kilts/loincloths. Black nipples visible on most butchers.
Butchery: Three of four oxen being slaughtered are mottled black and white with black outline, the fourth is white with red outline. All ear details and outlines, eye details, pupils and outlines black. Tongues orange-red, hooves yellow, horns outlined in black, tails black. Nostril of the white ox red. Two animals on right eyeball shaded in orange-red and orange-red anus, triangular area near anus brown on one and red on the other. Tail of second from right black with tip shaded in brown. Ribs of flayed ox orange-red and entrails spotted orange-red and white with red outline. Blood spilled from the cut is indicated in red paint on the hides of the animals below the knives cutting into the forelegs, and similarly on all of the knives used in the scene. Handle and blade of knives black, red splotches on all blades indicating blood from cuts. Whetstones (paint only) light blue with black rope.[132] Bowls to collect blood yellow. Binding ropes yellow with orange-red detail and outline.

---

pl. A; James, *Hieroglyphic Texts*, pl. 4:3; Weeks, *Cemetery G 6000*, fig. 35; Williams, *Perneb*, 70, Metropolitan Museum personal observation). The bowl is also held by standing figures.

131 Four or five men proceeding from a butchery scene with cuts of meat occur, e.g., in Lepsius, *Denkmäler* II, pls. 21, 67; *Saqqara Mastabas* 1, pls. 21, 23; Mohr, *Hetep-her-akhti*, figs. 36-38; Macramallah, *Idout*, pls. 15, 20; Simpson, *Western Cemetery*, pl. 32; idem, *Sekhem-ankh-Ptah*, pl. A.

132 Montet, on the basis that surviving paint is generally black, proposes flint or metal (*BIFAO* 7 [1909], 44), Griffith reports a "colour reminiscent of jade" (*Kahun and Gurob*, 36), and Ikram suggests a green or black basalt (*Choice Cuts*, 70-73).

Offering Bearers: Two of the forelegs carried by offering bearers mottled black and white, the third white with red outline (note in butchery scene three oxen are black and white and one is white). Two smaller cuts of meat red, one showing a white bone within the meat; binding and carrying ropes black. Spitted duck yellow with orange-red spots and outline. Tall jar red with black top on red pottery stand.

Commentary

Variations in height in this scene do not appear to be related to fitting a specific space. Each of the four butchers wielding the knife and their assistants are of similar size, but the two kneeling figures holding wide-mouth vessels are smaller in scale. They may be young boys, yet in the group skinning the ox a third and also central figure, gripping a knife and clearly a butcher, is likewise much smaller than his colleagues and comparable in size to the kneeling figures. In each instance where a third figure is added, that man is smaller than the other two. In addition, the two men leading the group carrying cuts of meat are equal in size, and taller than any of the butchers, but the third is slightly shorter and the fourth slightly shorter again, being similar in height to the butchers as well as wearing the same type of wig that exposes the ear.

CENTRE: MARSH ACTIVITIES

Pls. 15-16, 46

The central part of the east wall is fully occupied by a panel devoted to marsh activities. The decorated surface has an average width of 1.35m. and is equally divided into an upper and lower half, each .85m. high. The focal point is a scene in the upper half of the owner fowling, beneath which are three registers, .27m., .28m. and .30m. in height, depicting cattle fording, clapnet and dragnet scenes. This panel is not executed in relief and exhibits none of the detail, either in line or paint, as found, for example, in the registers of offerings on either side in the upper part of the wall or in the adjacent boat scenes in the lower part.

Colour

The surface of this section is thinly plastered. The entire fowling scene is very roughly and incompletely sketched, the figures and boats outlined in black paint but lacking evidence of any colour. The presumably unfinished and poorly preserved registers below retain very little detail. Some blue-grey ground remains in Registers 2-4 but colours are restricted to the faded red skin of the figures, wigs and some eye details in black, a few patches of white on loincloths, kilts and signal cloth. Cattle and papyrus boat outlines and binding in the fording scene, the blind and the birds of the clapnet and the rope of the dragnet, a crocodile and a few fish are discerned only as indistinct black lines. No details remain in the three water bands which now appear as faded ochre yellow but, with good lighting, minute traces of now crystallised blue paint can be seen in each band.

Register 1

The sketched figure of the tomb owner fowling is badly proportioned, the left arm and leg being much thicker than the right, and drawing of the face is particularly crude. He stands on the deck of a papyrus boat floating on a water band but there is no indication of a papyrus thicket. *Jrw-kȝ-Ptḥ* faces south, away from the entrance, his legs wide apart with the rear foot balancing on the toe. He wears a shoulder-length wig that exposes the ear, a broad collar and a short kilt. Two birds, grasped by the legs in the left hand, are held in front of his face as decoys and a throwstick is held high in his right hand. In front of him is a woman, smaller in scale but standing to the height of his chest, wearing a lappet wig, with both arms at her sides, the right hand holding a bird by the wing. Directly in front of her stands a smaller male figure, the body bisected by a vertical guideline and the legs no longer visible. Both arms hang at his side and the existing lines suggest that he wore a short wig and pointed kilt. At the stern of the boat is another smaller male figure wearing a short wig which exposes the ear and a kilt, with only the belt lines drawn. His legs are spread in a stance similar to that of *Jrw-kȝ-Ptḥ*, his left arm bent upwards and the right close to his body. Behind the tomb owner's boat, but facing in the opposite direction, is a small papyrus skiff with a single male figure standing with his legs apart and holding a long stick. This image is incomplete, with the front of the boat and the end of the stick missing.

Commentary

Presumably inspired by representations in the mortuary and valley temples of Userkaf and Sahure and perhaps especially the room of 'Seasons' in the sun temple of Neuserre, marsh scenes in general greatly increased in number in the second half of Dynasty 5.[133] They are most prevalent in the capital in the reigns of Djedkare, Unis and Teti; in Upper Egypt, while attested as early as Djedkare, the majority of examples date to Dynasty 6.[134] A fowling scene is first found in a private context in the reign of Sahure, attested in the Giza tomb of *Nswt-pw-nṯr* and possibly also at Saqqara in that of *Pr-sn*.[135] A representation of spear fishing in a private tomb appears in the reign of Neuserre or shortly after at Saqqara,[136] where, at about the same time, a composite scene of spear fishing and fowling is introduced in the tomb of *Nj-ꜥnḫ-H̱nmw* and *H̱nmw-ḥtp* on the east wall of the corridor in the rock-cut section.[137] Unusually spear fishing and fowling each appear a second time in this tomb, depicted prominently on either side of the entrance portico constructed as part of a third building stage.[138] A section of wall composed entirely around marsh activities is first encountered in the tomb of *Jj-mrjj* at Giza,[139] and groupings of marsh scenes in several registers similar to those of *Jrw-kȝ-Ptḥ* occur in tombs of other near contemporaries.[140]

There are a number of unusual features in the fowling scene of *Jrw-kȝ-Ptḥ*. First of all, his figure is proportionately much smaller than that of tomb owners in most

---

133 Harpur, *Decoration*, 190-96.
134 Ibid, 195, 355-67: Table 7.
135 Ibid, 186, 335-36: Table 6.18.
136 Mohr, *Hetep-her-akhti*, fig. 34.
137 Moussa - Altenmüller, *Nianchchnum*, pls. 74-75.
138 Ibid, pls. 4-5, figs. 5-6.
139 Harpur, *Decoration*, 187.
140 For example Mariette, *Mastabas*, 210; van de Walle, *Neferirtenef*, 92, pls. 1, 13; Simpson, *Kawab*, fig. 47; Schürmann, *Ii-nefret*, pl. 21; Moussa - Junge, *Two Craftsmen*, pls. 11-13; Ziegler, *Akhethetep*, 130-34.

fowling scenes, being only slightly taller than the adjacent butchers. Neither the shoulder-length wig exposing the ear nor the kilt he wears are usual attire. A wig which exposes the ear like that of *Jrw-kꜣ-Ptḥ* is attested in a fowling scene at Thebes in Dynasty 6.[141] Generally the tomb owner is depicted in both spear fishing and fowling scenes at the capital wearing a short wig, plain or curled, with or without a fillet, but always covering the ear. Shoulder-length wigs that cover the ears occur in spear fishing, fowling and composite scenes in the tomb of *Nj-ꜥnḫ-Ḫnmw* and *Ḫnmw-ḥtp*,[142] and in other composite scenes at Saqqara in the tombs of *Sḫntjw*, *Jrj.n-kꜣ-Ptḥ* and *Nfr-jrt.n.f*, not however in the fowling scene but only in the spear fishing scene,[143] as in the tomb of *Ḥtp-ḥr-ꜣḫtj*.[144] At Giza this type of wig is attested in a spear fishing scene and in a fowling scene.[145] These same scenes depict the tomb owner wearing a beard, which is not indicated for *Jrw-kꜣ-Ptḥ* nor for *Zꜣ-jb* at Giza.[146] It is to be noted that the Memphite examples cited are dated between the reigns of Neuserre and Unis. The sketched outline of *Jrw-kꜣ-Ptḥ*'s kilt does not appear to include the flap which projects beneath the short *šnḏwt* kilt worn by tomb owners in most spear fishing and fowling scenes. It resembles those worn by *Nj-ꜥnḫ-Ḫnmw* and *Ḫnmw-ḥtp* and by *Ḥtp-ḥr-ꜣḫtj*, which are short but with the end of the belt falling down in front.[147]

The two figures standing in front of *Jrw-kꜣ-Ptḥ* and facing the same direction are probably his wife and son.[148] The presence of family members in spear fishing and fowling scenes is not uncommon with female figures generally shown either kneeling on the deck close to or between the tomb owner's legs or standing near him. Where labels survive any female standing in a fowling boat in front of the tomb owner is designated as a wife.[149] While sons depicted in these scenes are often shown holding birds, women generally hold lotus flowers. However, rare examples of women holding birds in a similar manner are found in other fowling scenes at Saqqara at the beginning of Dynasty 6. In the recently discovered tomb of *Mr.f-nb.f*, two wives wearing long lappet wigs are depicted standing between

---

141 Saleh, *Tombs at Thebes*, pl. 12. A short wig with ears exposed occurs elsewhere in Upper Egypt in fowling scenes (Lepsius, *Denkmäler* II, pl. 106a; Davies, *Deir el-Gebrâwi* 2, pl. 3) but more commonly in spear fishing scenes (Kanawati, *El-Hawawish* 8, fig. 5; El-Khouli - Kanawati, *Quseir el-Amarna*, pl. 38; Blackman, *Meir* 5, pl. 28; Säve-Söderbergh, *Hamra Dom*, pl. 7).

142 Moussa - Altenmüller, *Nianchchnum*, figs. 5-6, pls. 4-5, 74-75.

143 Respectively, Moussa - Junge, *Two Craftsmen*, pls. 6, 12; van de Walle, *Neferirtenef*, pl. 1; Mohr, *Hetep-her-akhti*, fig. 34.

144 Mohr, *Hetep-her-akhti*, fig. 34. See also a spear fishing scene in the late Sixth Dynasty tomb of *ꜥnḫ.tj.fj* (Vandier, *Moꜥalla*, pl. 40).

145 *Kꜣ.j-m-ꜥnḫ* (Junker, *Gîza* 4, fig. 8); *Zꜣ-jb* (Roth, *Palace Attendants*, fig. 181).

146 Nor is a beard worn in the Upper Egyptian examples cited in n.141.

147 Respectively, Moussa - Altenmüller, *Nianchchnum*, figs. 5- 6, pls. 4-5, 74-75; Mohr, *Hetep-her-akhti*, fig. 34.

148 Harpur assumes that individuals standing in a boat in front of the tomb owner with their back to him, are family members (*Decoration*, 141).

149 An exception may occur in Upper Egypt of a female wearing a pigtail headdress who, although the inscription is not fully preserved, is probably a daughter (Säve-Söderbergh, *Hamra Dom*, pl. 8).

the fowler's legs and holding birds;[150] in the tomb of *Mrrw-k3.j* his wife, wearing a short wig and filet, stands in front of him in the fowling boat and holds a bird.[151] Two other scenes at Saqqara show a female wearing a pigtail, probably a daughter, standing behind the tomb owner, at least one on a baseline, and holding a bird.[152]

The height of the woman, whose head reaches *Jrw-kꜣ-Ptḥ*'s chest, may be another indication that she is his wife. Usually female figures, as well as most sons, in spear fishing and fowling scenes are relatively small in size, with the head of a standing woman not much above the tomb owner's thigh.[153] In the Memphite area a few other examples of wives who stand to the waist of the tomb owner or slightly higher are attested at Saqqara with a date in the latter part of Dynasty 5.[154] Most closely resembling the relative size in the tomb of *Jrw-kꜣ-Ptḥ* is a wife standing with her husband in a fowling boat in the closely contemporary tomb of *Nfr-jrt.n.f*.[155]

Additional family members or attendants are not frequently depicted at the stern of a papyrus boat where equipment is often placed, but rather on separate sub-registers near the boat. The active pose of the man standing behind the tomb owner, legs apart with one clenched fist raised to the height of his shoulder and the other near his hip, suggests that he may be punting, although the long pole either has disappeared or was never drawn. Punters appear in scenes of pleasure boating, *zšš wꜣḏ* or the hippopotamus hunt, but very rarely in spear fishing or fowling scenes.[156] Examples are found in a composite scene in the nearby tomb of *Nj-ꜥnḫ-Ḫnmw* and *Ḫnmw-ḥtp* dated to the reign of Neuserre, in the fowling scenes at Giza of *Jj-nfrt* in mid-Dynasty 5 and *Kꜣ.j-ḫr-Ptḥ* early in Dynasty 6, and on a fragment of spear fishing now in Berlin,[157] with possibly four examples in Upper Egypt.[158]

---

150 Myśliwiec, *Nowe oblicza Sakkary*, pls. 38, 49b. A single label of *ḥmt.f* written above their heads, presumably applies to both women, represented equal in height and each holding a leg of the tomb owner. The tomb owner is known to have a number of wives.

151 Duell, *Mereruka*, pls. 15, 17. In Upper Egypt a wife, wearing a short wig and filet, stands in front of the fowler, pointing with one hand and holding a bird in the other (Blackman, *Meir* 5, pl. 28).

152 Kaplony, *Methethi*, 10, 12; Quibell, *Saqqara* 1, pl. 20:4. Depicted in spear fishing scenes in Dynasty 6 in Upper Egypt are a daughter (Kanawati, *El-Hawawish* 2, fig. 18) and granddaughter (El-Khouli - Kanawati, *Quseir el-Amarna*, pl. 38) of the tomb owner, each on separate baselines and holding the bird before her face, a posture usually associated with males. Elsewhere a woman holding two birds accompanies a tomb owner viewing marsh activities (Blackman, *Meir* 5, pl. 13).

153 For example, Moussa - Altenmüller, *Nianchchnum*, figs. 5-6, pls. 4-5; Duell, *Mereruka*, pls. 9, 15; Kanawati - Abder-Raziq, *Teti Cemetery* 3, pl. 76.

154 Moussa - Junge, *Two Craftsmen*, pls. 6 (*Sḫntjw*, fragmentary), 12 (*Jrj.n-kꜣ-Ptḥ*); Lepsius, *Denkmäler* II, 60 (*Rꜥ-špss*). See also de Morgan, *Dahchour* 2, pl. 24 = CG 1775.

155 Van de Walle, *Neferirtenef*, pl. 1.

156 Harpur, *Decoration*, 141, 257.

157 Respectively, Moussa - Altenmüller, *Nianchchnum*, pls. 74-75; Schürmann, *Ii-nefret*, pl. 6; Kendall, *Studies Dunham*, fig. 11; Wreszinski, *Atlas* 1, pl. 377.

158 Punters appear in spear fishing scenes with probable dates of Pepy I (Varille, *Ni-ankh-Pepi*, pl. 9; Kanawati, *El-Hawawish* 6, fig. 3; vol. 8, fig. 5; vol. 9, fig. 15, the last three kneeling on a separate base line). A man with a long-handled oar at the stern of a fowling

The small papyrus skiff placed behind the fowling boat and facing away from the tomb owner is problematical. Although incomplete, it seems likely that the figure standing in this boat is engaged in a hippopotamus hunt.[159] The manner in which the long stick is held, with one outstretched arm raised high above the head, suggests the likelihood that it is a harpoon. Yet in other representations of a hippopotamus hunt the skiff is near the bow of the tomb owner's boat, facing in the same direction and generally with the same papyrus thicket as a background.[160]

Register 2

Oriented towards the entrance, in the opposite direction of the other marsh scenes, is a register depicting cattle fording water.[161] At the north end are five horned cattle[162] wading through the water with faint traces of what is possibly the head of a small calf in front of them. The mouth of the leading animal is not closed like the others, suggesting that it may have been calling, tongue protruding, to the calf behind.[163] Behind the cattle are two papyrus boats with three men, the most common number in fording scenes, in each. The kilts of the men in the prow of each boat cannot be distinguished and they may have been unclothed, the figures in the middle wear an abbreviated open kilt while those in the stern appear to wear a regular short kilt. All wear short wigs exposing the ears. In the first boat, a man kneels in the prow, sitting on his heels and holding a stick in his right hand. The figure behind him kneels on one leg and holds a stick or baton in his right hand while his left arm is raised and outstretched with the forefinger pointing in the gesture commonly assumed to be a protective one of warding off crocodiles.[164] A man kneeling in the stern with one knee raised is probably propelling the boat with a paddle or oar.[165] In the second boat a man in the prow kneels on one leg, the left extended behind him and his left arm stretched out in front of him. The other two men are depicted in the same manner as the second and third figures in the first boat, but the stick probably held by the man in the centre is no longer visible. The

---

boat being rowed in the late Dynasty 5 tomb of *Ḫw-ns* (Lepsius, *Denkmäler* II, pl. 106a) is probably not a punter (Harpur, *Decoration*, 362: Table 7 No. 26) but a helmsman.

159 For this theme see Vandier, *Manuel* 4, 773-81.

160 See for example, Lepsius, *Ergänzungsband,* pls. 11, 18; Duell, *Mereruka*, pls. 10-13; Macramallah, *Idout*, pl. 7; Munro, *Unas-Friedhof*, pl. 33; Kanawati - Abder-Raziq, *Teti Cemetery* 3, pl. 76; Schürmann, *Ii-nefret*, pls. 6, 21; in Upper Egypt, Blackman, *Meir* 5, pl. 30.

161 The theme is discussed by Vandier, *Manuel* 5, 96-128.

162 A herd of five or six cattle is quite normal but much larger numbers are attested, primarily from late Dynasty 5 to early Dynasty 6 (e.g., Lepsius, *Denkmäler* II, pls. 12b, 60; Junker, *Gîza* 11, fig. 67; Mohr, *Hetep-her-akhti*, fig. 33; Firth - Gunn, *Teti Pyr. Cem.* 2, pl. 52; Kanawati - Hassan, *Teti Cemetery* 2, pl. 37a).

163 The action is usually performed by a hornless mother(?) cow (Vandier, *Manuel* 5, 113-16) but an ox with horns is attested elsewhere at Saqqara (e.g., Lepsius, *Denkmäler* II, pl. 60; Kanawati - Abder-Raziq, *Teti Cemetery* 5, pls. 23, 55). While no certain examples are known at Giza the motif is found in Upper Egypt (e.g., Davies, *Deir el-Gebrâwi* 1, fig. 20; Kanawati, *El-Hawawish* 1, fig. 12).

164 See Montet, *Vie privée*, 69-72; Vandier, *Manuel* 5, 107-108, 117-18; Kanawati - Hassan, *Teti Cemetery* 2, 31-32. Attested at end of Dynasty 4, this motif is most common at the capital between mid Dynasty 5 and early Dynasty 6 (see Harpur, *Decoration*, 260, 355-60: Table 7.92).

165 Harpur notes this is an uncommon posture, the paddler usually depicted kneeling on both knees (ibid, 156). For a closely contemporary example see Lepsius, *Denkmäler* II, pl. 60.

only representation in the water band is the outline of a single crocodile beneath the boats. The unfinished and poorly preserved condition of this section of the east wall makes it difficult to judge whether additional aquatic life might have been included in the water band, but in a number of tombs at Saqqara dated from Djedkare to Pepy I a crocodile is the only marine animal shown.[166]

Commentary

A fording scene may be attested as early as Dynasty 3, but with few exceptions Memphite examples are dated between Neuserre and Pepy I.[167] Fording is often, as here, depicted in association with fishing and/or fowling in the marshes and with hippopotamus hunts. From mid-Dynasty 5 a calf is frequently included in cattle fording scenes,[168] generally either tied to the boat, held by a boatman in the stern or carried on the back of a man wading beside the herd. Some scenes with cattle emerging directly from a papyrus thicket lack an accompanying boat,[169] but usually cattle wading through a band of water are led by men in a small papyrus skiff. Two boats, one in front of and one behind the procession of cattle, are introduced perhaps as early as Neuserre in a scene in the tomb of *Kꜣ.j-m-nfrt* at Giza,[170] becoming more common towards the end of Dynasty 5 and early Dynasty 6, particularly at Saqqara.[171] Very rarely are two boats shown together at the front; an example attested at Giza is dated to Unis and another at Saqqara in the reign of Teti.[172] Equally rare is a boat following the herd rather than leading, although many scenes are too incomplete to be assured of no boat at the front. One instance is preserved on a fragment from Saqqara dated to the second half of

166 Mogensen, *Mastaba egyptién,* fig. 4, pl. 1; Davies, *Ptahhetep* 1, pl. 3; Épron - Wild, *Ti* 2, pl. 124; Duell, *Mereruka*, pls. 20-21; Kanawati - Hassan, *Teti Cemetery* 2, pl. 37a; Altenmüller, *Mehu*, pl. 39. The same is attested in late Dynasty 5 at Giza and in Upper Egypt (Smith, *HESPOK*, fig. 229; Lepsius, *Denkmäler* II, pl. 105b; Kanawati - McFarlane, *Deshasha*, pl. 46).

167 Harpur, *Decoration*, 348-50: Table 6.25. Scenes dated to early Dynasty 5 occur at Giza in the tombs of *Nswt-pw-nṯr* and *Nb-m-ꜣḫtj*; examples are found in Upper Egypt from the reign of Djedkare onward (ibid).

168 Ibid, 260. Early examples are *Kꜣ.j-m-nfrt* at Giza and *Ḥtp-ḥr-ꜣḫtj* at Saqqara (ibid, 355-363: Table 7.93).

169 For examples in the second half of Dynasty 5 see Moussa - Altenmüller, *Nefer*, pl. 5; Ziegler, *Akhethetep*, 131-32; Davies, *Ptahhetep* 2, pl. 14; Épron - Wild, *Ti* 2, pl. 114; Schürmann, *Ii-nefret*, pl. 21; in Dynasty 6 Junker, *Gîza* 4, fig. 8. These scenes generally show the cattle guided by a man walking in the water and depict no crocodile, although there is frequently a hippopotamus hunt nearby.

170 Hassan, *Gîza* 2, figs. 124, 140. Harpur dates the earliest to Djedkare (*Decoration*, 160).

171 Ibid, 195-96, 355-63: Table 7.95. E.g., Lepsius, *Denkmäler* II, pl. 60; Mogensen, *Mastaba egyptién*, fig. 4, pl. 1; Épron - Wild, *Ti* 2, pl. 124; Macramallah, *Idout*, pl. 7; Altenmüller, *Mehu*, pl. 39. Two boats are depicted in the Teti Cemetery in the tombs of three viziers who served that king (Duell, *Mereruka*, pls. 20-21; Kanawati - Hassan, *Teti Cemetery* 2, pl. 37a; Kanawati - Abder-Raziq, *Teti Cemetery* 5, pls. 23, 55). For examples in Upper Egypt see Davies, *Deir el-Gebrâwi* 2, pl. 20; Kanawati, *El-Hawawish* 1, fig. 12; vol. 2, fig. 22; vol. 4, fig. 18.

172 *Snḏm-jb/Mḥj* (Lepsius, *Ergänzungsband*, pl. 12) and *Kꜣ.j-gm-n.j* (Firth - Gunn, *Teti Pyr. Cem.* 2, pls. 7, 52).

Dynasty 5, and another in Upper Egypt towards the end of Dynasty 6, in both cases the cattle led by men wading in the water.[173]

The cattle fording scene of *Jrw-kꜣ-Ptḥ* is unusual in lacking a boat or a man guiding the herd through water and apparently unique in representing two boats following the cattle. Like the fowling scene above, the north end of this register appears incomplete, a result of either originally misjudging the available space or possibly later damage by the addition of the adjacent niche with its unfinished statue. Yet the decoration of the two registers below appears to have been planned to fit the present length of the register. It is difficult to determine if the fording scene was originally designed to include a man or a boat with the calf at north end of the register. Perhaps misjudgement of space resulted in two boats following rather than one leading and one following. It remains possible that the artist erroneously drew the cattle facing away from the boats which normally lead them.

Register 3

The clapnet scene includes a signalman, five haulers and, standing behind them, a supervisor in a pointed kilt. As far as can be determined none of the other figures wear a kilt or loin cloth. The outline of the hexagonal net is clear, but little detail is preserved of the birds caught in the net, and even less of any birds and/or water vegetation beneath. A painted vertical red line at the left may indicate a peg to secure the net.[174] The men participating in the capture are hidden from the net and birds by a hide, a stylised column of either reeds or papyrus. In the centre of the hide an oval shape is clearly outlined in black. There seems to be no identical parallel but it may be noted that in two tombs at Saqqara dated to early Dynasty 6 a butterfly is represented on the hide in a similar position.[175]

In front of the hide is a signalman, standing upright with his legs wide apart. His back is to the net, both body and face oriented (south) towards the haulers in front of him, and his arms are outstretched with the hands holding the ends of the signal cloth lying across his shoulders.[176] The cord of the clapnet is being pulled by the five haulers facing him,[177] all but the last, who is depicted as balding, wearing a short cap wig with the ear exposed. The first hauler stands with his legs wide apart, the right knee bent, and leans forward with both arms stretched out in front of him to grasp the cord; although the lines are not visible, he probably has an abbreviated shoulder. The four men behind him are broad shouldered with both arms extended forward to hold the cord in front of them just below waist level. Behind the haulers, and also facing the net, stands a man with a balding head who wears a pointed kilt. Overseers sometimes appear at one side of a clapnet scene and, while frequently shown balding, generally wear the herdsman's kilt and lean

---

173 Respectively, Borchardt, *Denkmäler* 2, 18, pl. 61 = CG 1557; Kanawati, *El-Hawawish* 7, fig. 32.

174 See, for example, Barsanti, *ASAE* 1 [1900], fig. 9; compare Épron - Wild, *Ti* 2, pl. 122.

175 *Mḥw* (Altenmüller, *Mehu*, pls. 7-8, 31b, 34a) and *Ḥzj* (Kanawati - Abder-Raziq, *Teti Cemetery* 5, pls. 22, 55).

176 This pose of the signalman is attested from early Dynasty 4 (Harpur, *Decoration*, 142).

177 The number of haulers in individual scenes is commonly between three and five. In the tomb of *Ptḥ-ḥtp* II, a double scene shows seven seated haulers in one register and above it another six lying on their backs (Paget - Pirie, *Ptah-hetep*, fig. 32).

on or hold a staff.[178] None are known to be represented with the posture of the man in *Jrw-kꜣ-Ptḥ*'s clapnet scene whose right arm touches his left shoulder and the left bends to rest across his chest.[179]

Commentary

Several clapnet scenes are documented at Meidum at the beginning of Dynasty 4 and at Giza at the end of Dynasty 4, but the vast majority in the Memphite area date from mid-Dynasty 5 to early Dynasty 6.[180] A stylised hide is first included in the earliest attested clapnet scene at Saqqara, in the tomb of *Wr-jr.n-Ptḥ* dated to Neferirkare-Neferefre.[181] In any given clapnet scene the figures of haulers usually have virtually identical body and arm positions, although a head may be turned backwards. Seldom does the posture of any one differ from the others as does the first hauler in *Jrw-kꜣ-Ptḥ*'s tomb, the few exceptions occurring mainly in the period Neuserre-Unis.[182] Unlike the haulers in most clapnet scenes, those in the tomb of *Jrw-kꜣ-Ptḥ* appear almost static with little indication of action, depicted in a normal striding posture with both feet flat on the ground but leaning very slightly backwards. This differs from the more usual and active forward-leaning pose with legs wide apart and the heel of the rear foot raised, but haulers with feet flat on the ground are attested in a few tombs at Saqqara between late Dynasty 5 and early Dynasty 6.[183] It also differs from the rare examples documented at Saqqara in the same period of haulers bending forward from the waist but leaning backwards with stiff legs close together and heels digging into the ground.[184] In Dynasty 6 haulers leaning back stiffly without bending appear in the tomb of *Sšm-nfr/Jwfj* in the Unis Cemetery,[185] but are more frequently found in Upper Egypt.[186]

Register 4

The bottom register of the panel depicting a dragnet scene is poorly preserved and few details remain.[187] The men in this register are not as tall as those in the clapnet

---

178 E.g., Lepsius, *Ergänzungsband*, pl. 14; Hassan, *Gîza* 2, fig. 240; Weeks, *Cemetery G 6000*, pl. 40; Moussa - Altenmüller, *Nianchchnum*, fig. 12, pl. 31; Munro, *Unas-Friedhof*, pl. 33; Kanawati - Hassan, *Teti Cemetery* 2, pl. 42; Altenmüller, *Mehu*, pl. 7.

179 Note however a man standing at one side of the dragnet scene in the mastaba of *3ḫt-ḥtp* who similarly places his right hand on his left shoulder although his left hand hangs by his side holding a cord or rope (Ziegler, *Akhethetep*, 83, 134).

180 Harpur, *Decoration*, 339-40: Table 6.19.

181 Ibid, 188, 258.

182 Ibid, 143. E.g., Lepsius, *Denkmäler* II, pl. 43a; Épron - Wild, *Ti* 2, pl. 122; Hassan, *Gîza* 5, fig. 173; Mohr, *Hetep-her-akhti*, fig. 25; Moussa - Altenmüller, *Nefer*, pl. 6.

183 Capart, *Rue de tombeaux* 2, pl. 86; Ziegler, *Akhethetep*, 132-33; Altenmüller, *Mehu*, pls. 7, 34a; Kanawati - Hassan, *Teti Cemetery* 2, pl. 42; Kanawati - Abder-Raziq, *Teti Cemetery* 5, pls. 21, 55. For an example in Upper Egypt see Kanawati - McFarlane, *Deshasha*, pl. 46.

184 Mohr, *Hetep-her-akhti*, fig. 25; Épron - Wild, *Ti* 2, pls. 120, 122; Lloyd et al., *Saqqâra Tombs* 2, pl. 8. The stance is also found in Upper Egypt in late Dynasty 5 (Kanawati - McFarlane, *Deshasha*, pl. 33) and Dynasty 6 (Blackman, *Meir* 4, pl. 8).

185 Barsanti, *ASAE* 1 [1900], fig. 9.

186 Petrie, *Dendereh*, pl. 5; Saleh, *Tombs at Thebes*, pl. 18; Blackman, *Meir* 4, pl. 13; Kanawati, *El-Hagarsa* 3, pl. 35.

187 The register is neither a continuation at the left of the clapnet scene above nor does it depict at the right butchers and a bound ox as suggested by de Rachewiltz (*Irw-k3-Ptḥ*, 17).

scene above as some of the space was required for the water band beneath, which retains a portion of the net and a few fish. Pulling on the rope of the net are ten haulers divided into two equal groups on either side of an overseer standing in the middle.[188] The haulers are represented in virtually identical poses, leaning forward from the hips on flat feet spaced widely apart with the knee of the front leg bent and the back leg straight. All haulers are depicted with abbreviated shoulders and both arms extended forward in the same manner to grasp the rope with the near hand behind the far hand. The man at each end bends further forward to gather the ropes of the net from the water. At least six of the ten are balding and the ears of all are exposed. The lines of a belt are preserved on several figures, with shoulder straps visible on two of these, and the man at the north end wears a short open kilt. In the centre of the scene stands an overseer, facing in the same direction as the fowling tomb owner and the dragnet signalman in the registers above. He is depicted as a portly, balding figure wearing a knee-length pointed kilt, with an abbreviated shoulder and leaning on a staff in a flat foot posture.

Commentary

Dragnet scenes, like clapnet scenes, are attested at Meidum and Giza in Dynasty 4 but are most prevalent at the capital from mid-Dynasty 5 to early Dynasty 6.[189] The abbreviated shoulder, an artistic convention common when representing workers in action, is frequently used for haulers and occasionally for overseers in dragnet scenes from the reign of Neuserre.[190] At Giza an overseer with an abbreviated shoulder stands among the haulers in the slightly earlier tomb of *Jj-mrjj* and at the end of Dynasty 5 in that of *Sšm-nfr* IV, although neither leans on a staff.[191] At Saqqara an overseer in the centre leaning on a staff is depicted with an abbreviated shoulder late in Dynasty 5 in the tombs of *Nfr-jrt.n.f* and *Ṯjj*, and early in Dynasty 6 in that of *Mḥw*.[192] Not all details are preserved in the scene of *Nfr-jrt.n.f*, but those of *Ṯjj* and *Mḥw* show, like that of *Jrw-kȝ-Ptḥ*, a balding and portly man. Corpulent overseers become more common from Neuserre onward[193] but are not frequent in dragnet scenes. An early example is found in the Unis causeway tomb of *Nj-ꜥnḫ-Ḫnmw* and *Ḫnmw-ḥtp*,[194] not, however, with an abbreviated shoulder or leaning on a staff as in the tombs of *Jrw-kȝ-Ptḥ*, *Ṯjj* and *Mḥw*.[195] Where details remain, the dragnet scenes cited above show the overseer

---

188 An overseer first appears in the middle of the dragnet scene in the reign of Sahure (Harpur, *Decoration*, 259). Haulers most frequently number between six and twelve, but in the tomb of *Mrrw-kȝ.j* are scenes with 18, 23 and 28 (Duell, *Mereruka*, pls. 43, 55; Wreszinski, *Atlas* 1, pl. 95 = Vandier, *Manuel* 5, pl. 4, fig. 36).

189 Harpur, *Decoration*, 341-43: Table 6.20. The theme is discussed by Vandier, *Manuel* 5, 559-601; Brewer - Friedman, *Fish and Fishing*, 42-46.

190 Harpur, *Decoration*, 145-46, 258.

191 Respectively, Weeks, *Cemetery G 6000*, pl. 40; Junker, *Gîza* 11, fig. 66. These appear to be the only examples preserved in dragnet scenes at Giza.

192 Respectively, van de Walle, *Neferirtenef*, pl. 13; Épron - Wild, *Ti* 2, pl. 123; Altenmüller, *Mehu*, pls. 31a, 35b. For rare examples preserved in Upper Egypt in Dynasty 6 see Blackman, *Meir* 4, pl. 8; vol. 5, pl. 30.

193 Harpur, *Decoration*, 146.

194 Moussa - Altenmüller, *Nianchchnum*, pl. 31, fig. 12.

195 Other examples appear at Abusir (Lepsius, *Ergänzungsband*, pl. 40d) and Dahshur (Borchardt, *Denkmäler* 2, 192, pl. 103 = CG 1772), but none is preserved in Upper Egypt.

clad, as is common, in a herdsman's kilt rather than the pointed one found in *Jrw-kȝ-Ptḥ*'s tomb. However a pointed kilt is worn by an overseer standing to one side of the net in the tomb of *Ḫʿ.f-Ḫwfw* II and a plain kilt appears in the tombs of *Sḫm-kȝ-Rʿ*, *Ḫʿ.f-Rʿ-ʿnḫ* and *ȝḫt-ḥtp*.[196] *Sḫm-kȝ-Rʿ* is dated to Sahure and the other four in the reign of Neuserre or slightly later. In the scene of *Jrw-kȝ-Ptḥ* an object resting on the back of the overseer, and possibly hanging over his shoulder, is difficult to identify but resembles a cloth(?) placed over the shoulder of an overseer in the closely contemporary tomb of *Ḥtp-ḥr-ȝḫtj* at Saqqara as well as in those of *Jj-nfrt* and *Sšm-nfr* IV at Giza and *Snfrw-jn-jšt.f* at Dahshur which are dated in the period late Dynasty 5-early Dynasty 6.[197]

The dragnet scene of *Jrw-kȝ-Ptḥ* conveys little sense of motion, whereas this theme is usually among the liveliest of the Old Kingdom repertoire with the figures showing a great diversity in posture and action.[198] The movement of each group of haulers is normally oriented towards the centre of the scene, yet figures within the same group may move in or face different directions, heads sometimes looking back, and may bend far over from the waist, lean stiffly back on the heels or even kneel. The representation in *Jrw-kȝ-Ptḥ*'s tomb is quite exceptional in several aspects: there is no variation in the posture of the haulers, nine of the ten men face the same direction and all stand with feet flat on the ground. In other dragnet scenes, where sufficient detail remains, it is unusual to find all haulers in a flat foot posture. Rare examples are attested at Memphis in the second half of Dynasty 5,[199] and others in Upper Egypt, primarily in Dynasty 6.[200] Some of these give a similar impression of stiffness but others display a rather greater sense of action. A strap worn over the shoulder by one or more haulers to assist with pulling in the net appears in the reign of Neuserre.[201] Attested at Saqqara in the tomb of *Nfr* and *Kȝ.j-ḥȝ.j* and at Giza in that of *Ḫʿ.f-Ḫwfw* II,[202] the motif occurs frequently in later dragnet scenes.

---

196 Respectively, Simpson, *Kawab*, fig. 47; Lepsius, *Denkmäler* II, pls. 42a, 9; Ziegler, *Akhethetep*, 133. Similar examples are attested in Upper Egypt (e.g., Varille, *Ni-ankh-Pepi*, pl. 6; Blackman, *Meir* 5, pls. 13, 30; Kanawati, *El-Hawawish* 2, fig. 22).

197 Respectively, Mohr, *Hetep-her-akhti*, 58-60, fig. 29; Schürmann, *Ii-nefret*, pl. 11; Junker, *Gîza* 11, fig. 66; Borchardt, *Denkmäler* 2, 192, pl. 103 = CG 1772. Not a very common detail (Harpur, *Decoration*, 171, n.122), the motif also occurs in scenes of fording (e.g., Altenmüller, *Mehu*, pl. 77) and the claptrap (e.g., Davies, *Sheikh Saïd*, pl. 12).

198 Harpur, *Decoration*, 145-46. See also Vandier, *Manuel* 5, 573-79; Fischer, *JNES* 18 [1959], 241-42.

199 *Ḫʿ.f-Rʿ-ʿnḫ* (Lepsius, *Denkmäler* II, pl. 9), *Ḫww-wr* (Hassan, *Gîza* 5, fig. 104) and probably *Sḫm-kȝ.j* (Simpson, *Western Cemetery*, fig. 4) at Giza, and *ȝḫt-ḥtp* (Ziegler, *Akhethetep*, 133) at Saqqara.

200 Lepsius, *Denkmäler* II, pl. 106; Varille, *Ni-ankh-Pepi*, pl. 6; Davies, *Deir el-Gebrâwi* 1, pl. 4; vol. 2, pl. 5; Blackman, *Meir* 5, pls. 13, 30; Saleh, *Theban Tombs*, pl. 11; Kanawati, *El-Hawawish* 1, fig. 12; vol. 2, fig. 22; vol. 8, fig. 13.

201 Harpur, *Decoration*, 189, 259.

202 Respectively, Moussa - Altenmüller, *Nefer*, pl. 4; Simpson, *Kawab*, fig. 47.

SOUTH, UPPER PART: SEATED TOMB OWNER AND OFFERINGS

Pls. 3a, 17, 19-21, 47, 49

The upper part of the south end of the east wall, almost a duplicate in reverse of the scene at the north end of the same wall, depicts a male figure seated before a table and two registers of piled offerings. The scene covers a total width of 3.65m. The seated figure, immediately above the serdab, occupies a height of .70m.; the piled food offerings, placed above the horizontal inscription, have a height of .46m. at the south and .49m. at the north and are divided into two registers of almost equal height. Most of the representations of food offerings are well-preserved but the plaster has fallen from the scene of the seated figure which retains little detail. In front of the face very faint traces remain of what may have been a short inscription giving a name and title(s). However, it may be assumed that the figure represents the tomb owner, *Jrw-kꜣ-Ptḥ*. The indistinct lines indicate that he was seated on a chair like that at the north end, with a low cushion and showing no front leg, but in this instance the back leg is that of a lion and rests on a socle.[203] He also similarly wears a shoulder length wig and beard(?), but a plain kilt rather than a pointed one, and both arms, with empty hands palm down, are extended towards the faint outlines of an offering table. A ewer and basin are placed beneath the table which probably held three conical loaves,[204] rather than the usual half-loaves.

Although similar in composition, the painted details of the piled offerings depicted at the south end are better executed than those at the north end which are, however, balanced more artistically. That the offerings were arranged to face the tomb owner can be detected by the direction in which the calves' heads face, here to the south and at the opposite end to the north. Little plaster is preserved at the beginning of the narrower upper register and few lines can be discerned in front of two low wooden tables holding jars. Placed on the first are two ewers and basins with a spouted jar between them and on the second two carinated stone bowls with fancy tied covers. Under the first table is a hexagonal loaf and a wide-mouthed carinated jar with a spout and under the second are two loaves, one conical and the second elongated and lying on a flat tray. Next is a low stand supporting a curved tray of basketry that holds a lettuce and loaves; on each side of the stand are two more loaves, one pair laid horizontally on a tray. Adjacent are four tall jars, two elongated oval shapes placed on pottery stands and, separated by a conical loaf, two more elaborate jars with collars. These are followed by an asymmetrically

---

203 A common form of socle (Cherpion, *Mastabas et hypogées*, 37, 40, fig. 21: Criterion 13.c).

204 Tables holding various food offerings are placed by Cherpion primarily between mid-Dynasty 4 and mid-Dynasty 5 (ibid, 49-50, 171-72: Criterion 22), but the motif is also known in Dynasty 6 (e.g. Junker, *Gîza* 6, fig. 62, pl. 16C; Simpson, *Qar and Idu*, figs. 17-18). For Fifth Dynasty examples see e.g. Lepsius, *Denkmäler* II, pls. 10-11, 33; Borchardt, *Denkmäler* 1, pl. 47 = CG 1533; Mariette, *Mastabas*, 200; Reisner, *Giza*, fig. 259; Junker, *Gîza* 10, fig. 44; James, *Hieroglyphic Texts*, pl. 28; Firth - Gunn, *Teti Pyr. Cem.* 1, pl. 62; Badawy, *Iteti*, fig. 11; Davies, *Sheikh Saïd*, pl. 4; Roth, *Palace Attendants*, pl. 190. Examples of various types of table offerings are illustrated in Junker, *Gîza* 12, fig. 3 and Hassan, *Gîza* 5, fig. 16.

shaped basket[205] on a wicker stand which is filled with pomegranates, grapes, vegetables and lotus flowers. To one side of the stand are two elongated loaves laid on a flat tray, and on the other side is a conical loaf. Next is a basketry stand and tray laden with different types of loaves and a bunch of grapes and beneath the tray are four loaves and a small container. The register ends with another low wooden table holding lettuces and other items which are no longer distinguishable.

The lower register is dominated by five basketry containers, three slightly concave on tall wicker stands and two boat-shaped placed on low tables on short stands, probably of pottery. The simpler baskets are filled primarily with loaves and the two boat-shaped baskets with fruit and vegetables. The right end of the lower register is poorly preserved but the first object appears to be a tall jar adjacent to a basketry tray on a stand holding four loaves. Another, larger basketry tray on a higher stand holds four loaves and a bunch of onions; beneath, on the right, is a calf's head and, on the left, two small containers supporting a flat tray on which rest two elongated loaves. Next are two tall oval-shaped jars on pottery stands. The third basket is boat-shaped and placed on a low round table with an upturned rim which rests on a short stand. The basket is filled with pomegranates piled on either side of two small containers which support a small woven tray holding three loaves of bread and a bunch of grapes. Laid on the table on either side of the basket is a loaf of bread, and beneath the table are a number of small loaves and two containers filled, probably, with grapes. Next is an elaborate stone bowl with a cover placed on a stone jar-stand between one large and one small loaf. Another basketry tray on a wicker stand holds four loaves, some onions and a bunch of grapes. Beneath it on the right is a carinated and footed bowl with a cover draped with two bunches of grapes, and on the left is a second calf's head. A group of four tall jars, three on jar-stands, is composed of an elaborate jar with a collar on each side of two elongated oval-shaped jars in the middle. The last basket has the same form as the third and, like it, is placed on a low pottery table. In the centre of the basket, between two marrows and bound leeks,[206] are three small containers which support a flat woven tray on which are arranged pomegranates. Two elongated loaves lie horizontally on pottery trays on either side of the table stand, and at the left is a large conical loaf. The register ends, as does that at the southern end of the wall, with a large covered bowl on a stand, similar to that in the middle of this register but here represented only in painted black outline.

Colour

Low tables in top register black with yellow markings; woven baskets and trays of various shapes (3 top register, 5 bottom register) white with red detail and outline; flat trays red; one tray under chest in top register orange-red; stands in bottom register, one red, one (with opening) orange-red.
Jars top register, from right: Two ewers and basins blue, spouted jar red, low carinated bowl with spout under chest red. Two carinated stone containers white with blue and black detail, black outline; covers yellow outlined in red, ties blue

205 For example Murray, *Saqqara* 1, pls. 21-23; Petrie - Murray, *Memphite Chapels*, pl. 13; Épron - Wild, *Ti* 1, pls. 52-54; Simpson, *Western Cemetery*, fig. 32; idem, *Kayemnofret*, pl. C; Moussa - Altenmüller, *Nefer*, pl. 25b; Roth, *Palace Attendants*, pl. 141.

206 For this identification see Brewer et al., *Plants and Animals*, 66, fig. 6.3.

with black detail and outline. Two tall oval jars red with black tops, on red stands. One large jar red with blue collar and red tie; second large jar black with sections at top blue, on red stand. Small container beneath woven tray red, contents yellow.
Jars bottom register, from right: Three small containers under wicker trays red, one with blue contents (probably grapes). Two tall oval jars, lower part red and top black, on red stands. Two small containers supporting tray in basket red; two small containers below tray red, holding blue grapes. Large stone container, bowl and stand white with black markings, lashing black on white, cover yellow with red outline, black detail on tie. Small footed and carinated container red, cover yellow with red outline, tie white with black outline. Tall jar red with blue collar around middle. Two tall jars red with black tops, on red stands. Tall jar black with blue band in upper part, on red stand. Three small containers supporting tray in woven basket, two red and centre one blue. Large (stone?) container on stand white with all detail and outline in black paint, only right side of container carved.
Loaves, all outlined in red: Conical loaves yellow with brown shading at top, first loaf at north end of each register plain yellow; elongated loaves placed horizontally on or under trays and chests yellow with brown shaded top and white blotches in lower part; rectangular loaves white with yellow and dark ochre (brown) or dark red markings, red outline; hexagonal loaves white with horizontal red and yellow detail, red outline.
Lettuces light green; pomegranates yellow with orange-red details and stems, dark red outline; leeks light green, black outline; marrows light green, black outline; onion bulbs white with orange-red stripes and black tops; grapes blue; lotus stem red, flower green and blue. Calves' heads white with black spots, black eye detail, red line at neck (where severed?).

SOUTH, LOWER PART: BOAT TRANSPORT

Pls. 2, 17-18, 47-48

The lower part of the east wall adjacent to the marsh scenes is occupied by eight boats in four registers of two each, six travelling ships and two cargo boats. The panel is 1.50m. wide, the upper two registers with ships under sail have a height of .39m. the third is .31m., while the bottom register which no longer preserves the .06m. high water band of the others, is .24m. high. The design of their wooden hulls is typical of the Old Kingdom, flat-bottomed with the stern at a more acute angle and slightly higher than the bow.[207] All of the boats are portrayed with the bow to the right, that is, progressing to the south, except those in the third register powered by oar which travel, with the current, northward.[208] The boats on this register are on the same water band as the adjacent dragnet scene. While the boats themselves are quite well-preserved, no detail remains in the bands of water beneath them.

Four large boats under sail in the upper two registers are depicted moving south with the north wind. The second boat in the top register is papyriform, the bow

---

207 See Landström, *Ships*, figs. 105, 108; Jones, *Boats*, 36.

208 It is quite usual for ships under sail and oar to be oriented in opposite directions, e.g., Hassan, *Gîza* 5, fig. 104; Épron - Wild, *Ti* 1, pl. 49; Steindorff, *Catalogue Walters*, pl. 50; Moussa - Junge, *Two Craftsmen*, pl. 8; Ziegler, *Akhethetep*, 138-43.

and stern in the shape of papyrus bundles and the lashing to bind them represented at each end of the hull. All four sailing boats are similarly outfitted and rigged.[209] They have a tall bi-pod mast, two legs strengthened by crossbars and rounded at the top.[210] The mast, placed forward of amidships, is stabilized by a forestay,[211] a standing backstay and additional backstays or shrouds which stretch from the upper part of the mast to the deck. Each mast carries a tall sail with the trapezoidal shape typical of Dynasty 5 which is slightly narrower at the bottom so that the foot of the sail remains within the beam of the boat.[212] The sail, attached to a straight upper yard and a lower yard or boom, is manoeuvred by two braces secured to each end of the upper yardarm. The lower yard, with lashing detail similar to that of the top yard, rests on the deck aft of the mast as is clear on three of the four boats.[213]

Shelter is provided by a deckhouse, with a roof strong enough to support the weight of one or more crew, and a flat awning which extends from the mast to the stern. The sheltered area is divided into three sections; the deckhouse or cabin in the central part is enclosed by plaited or woven matting while the sides of the sections at either end, supported by (pairs of) posts, are open. The posts at either end of the deckhouse have a zig-zag lashing, while those at the stern show a pattern of checks and horizontal bands. The difference in decoration may suggest that at the stern there was hung a length of the same matting material which enclosed the deckhouse.

The tomb owner, although not named, is portrayed on each of the sailing boats, standing and facing the prow in the open area in front of the deckhouse, just behind the mast. He wears a pointed kilt and in three instances a shoulder-length wig and once, in the second boat of the top register, a short wig exposing the ear.[214] A collar is preserved on one figure of the owner in each of the top two registers. In the first boat in each register he holds a staff in his left hand while his right arm hangs by his side with the hand clenched, a folded cloth preserved in the first boat of the top register. In the second boat in each register he is shown leaning on his staff. Standing forward of the mast in three of the four boats is a man who,

---

209 For a reconstruction of a typical sailing ship of Dynasties 4 and 5 see Landström, *Ships*, figs. 119-21.

210 Masts are usually depicted as two-legged until probably early in Dynasty 6 (Jones, *Boats*, 39) when both bi-pod and single pole masts are found in the Saqqara tombs of *Mrrw-kꜣ.j* (Duell, *Mereruka*, pls. 140-144) and *Mḥw* (Altenmüller, *Mehu*, pls. 19, 22a). Both types also appear together in Upper Egypt in Dynasty 6 (e.g., Davies, *Deir el-Gebrâwi* 2, pl. 7; Blackman, *Meir* 5, pl. 22, Kanawati, *El-Hawawish* 1, fig. 9; vol. 2, fig. 19).

211 The forestay first appeared at the beginning of Dynasty 5, simultaneously with a higher mast and larger sail area (Boreaux, *Nautique*, 357-58; Jones, *Boats*, 37).

212 Landström, *Ships*, 43, 46, fig. 120. A shorter, rectangular sail appears early in Dynasty 6, the result of changes in ship design which include equal length yards, a shorter mast and halyards to keep the lower yard above the deck (e.g., Duell, *Mereruka*, pls. 140, 142-44; Borchardt, *Denkmäler* 2, 240, pl. 50B = CG 1536; Davies, *Deir el-Gebrâwi* 2, pl. 7).

213 Resting on the deck, the lower yard is frequently hidden behind the bulwark or crew (Vandier, *Manuel* 5, 797).

214 A short wig worn by tomb owners on boats is not uncommon, but encountered less frequently than the shoulder-length wig.

wearing a pointed kilt like the tomb owner and portrayed facing him in attitudes of deference, may be an official.[215]

The crew represented on each ship numbers between 12 and 15. Where the outlines are clear the men are depicted with short wigs exposing the ears and wearing a belt with three flaps of fabric falling in front. Standing at the bow and looking straight ahead is a lookout or pilot. He holds upright in his left hand a forked staff, which may also be used to sound the depth, and in his right hand a cord, possibly used in signalling. Seated on the lower yard behind him and facing the stern are three, in one case four, crew members who were probably responsible for adjusting the heavy lower yard which rested on the deck.[216]

Amidships behind the tomb owner are depicted rowers. The first and fourth boats each hold five rowers and the second and third six, and it is probable that each had an unseen counterpart on the far side of the deckhouse.[217] As the boat is under sail they are shown at rest, facing the prow and the tomb owner, with their arms in front of them and their hands, presumably, resting on their laps. Only the upper body shows above the gunwale; their seats on the deck level are not visible. The oars are raised above the water and, as seen on the second boat in each register, suspended in slings of rope or leather which pass through narrow slots in the bulwark.[218] These rowlocks are correctly positioned on the boat in the upper register, while those of the boat beneath are lower down the shaft of the oar.[219] In each ship the number of oars exceeds the number of rowers, although it may be presumed that the sailors on the foredeck responsible for the lower yard would have assumed positions as rowers when the sail was lowered. Ten oars are depicted on three of the ships while perhaps 13 can be distinguished among the confusing overlap of relief edges and painted lines on the first boat in the second register.[220]

---

215 See Vandier, *Manuel* 5, 865-67. The figure(s) depicted in attitude of obeisance or holding a scroll of papyrus is usually the only person on board other than the tomb owner shown wearing a kilt. Sometimes designated by name and/or title, he is occasionally identified as a scribe and may be reporting to or receiving orders from the owner.

216 Ibid, 853-54. As shown here, several men are often seated on the yard, perhaps to prevent it lifting with strong wind (Landström, *Ships*, 43), and are usually shown facing the stern, perhaps to more easily respond to the directions of the helmsmen. Forward facing figures are less common but attested at Giza (e.g., Lepsius, *Denkmäler* II, pl. 22; Junker, *Gîza* 2, fig. 22; vol. 4, pls. 3-5, 7; Hassan, *Gîza* 5, fig. 104) and Saqqara (Mogensen, *Mastaba egyptién*, fig. 9; Moussa - Altenmüller, *Nefer*, pl. 16; Ziegler, *Akhethetep*, 142-43). Two figures face forward and two backward on each of two sailing ships in the tomb of *Snfrw-jn-jšt.f* (de Morgan, *Dahchour* 2, pl. 19).

217 Pairs of sailors are clearly depicted sitting on the lower yard in the tomb of *Nj-ʿnḫ-H̱nmw* and *H̱nmw-ḥtp* (Moussa - Altenmüller, *Nianchchnum*, fig. 10, pl. 25).

218 Boreaux, *Nautique*, 338-39; Jones, *Boats*, 38. Rowlocks for the oars are preserved in the Saqqara tombs of *H̱nmw-ḥtp* (Petrie - Murray, *Memphite Chapels*, pl. 17:2), *Ṯjj* (Épron - Wild, *Ti* 1, pls. 22-24) and *3ḫt-ḥtp* (Ziegler, *Akhethetep*, 138-39); the holes to attach the oarlocks are clearly represented in Ziegler, *Akhethetep*, 143 and Épron - Wild, *Ti* 2, pl. 129 (hull under construction).

219 Similarly, Mogensen, *Mastaba egyptién*, fig. 10.

220 Many more oars than crew are often depicted on boats under sail, for example Épron - Wild, *Ti* 1, pls. 47-49; Moussa - Altenmüller, *Nefer*, pl. 17; Altenmüller, *Mehu*, pl. 19a.

Standing among the rowers in three of the boats is a man with legs widespread and arms outstretched. He faces the helmsmen at the stern and may act as a signalman, relaying instructions or directions. In the first boat of the second register this crewman holds a sceptre-like baton.[221] The boat is guided by two helmsmen standing at the stern under the awning. Each grips a long-handled steering oar, both shown on the same side of the boat, secured by a long cord tied to the butt of the oar and attached to semi-circular slings on the bulwark.[222] Seated on the roof of the deckhouse is a man who holds in each hand one of the two rope braces attached to either end of the yardarm by which the sail is adjusted according to the strength and direction of the wind.[223]

The third register, which has less height than the upper two, shows two boats under oar and moving in the opposite direction, north with the current. The leading boat has a shape similar to the four sailing boats above, but the bulwark projects slightly beyond the stern of the hull. The bow of the second ship has the shape of an animal head, usually taken to be a hedgehog,[224] and the stern is slightly rounded. Each boat has a deckhouse constructed and decorated like those on the sailing boats above but placed further forward amidships and the awning extends from the forward edge of the bulwark to the stern.

The boats in this register are manned by two lookouts standing in the prow, a signalman, four oarsmen and two helmsmen at the stern. Each of the lookouts holds a forked pole in the right hand except the first in the leading boat whose right arm is missing, but who grasps a cord or cloth in the left hand. On both boats the tomb owner stands facing forward under the awning in front of the deckhouse, wearing a pointed kilt and again depicted in the unusual manner of holding his staff in front of him. In the lead boat an official wearing a kilt is facing him, bowing forward. The position of his partly-preserved arms indicates that he may have held a papyrus.[225] Behind the tomb owner the rowers are shown seated above the deck level, facing the stern and gripping the oars. With both arms stretched out in front

---

221 For commentary on this baton held on boats see Fischer, *MMJ* 13 [1978], 16, fig. 22a.

222 Boreaux, *Nautique*, 387-95; Landström, *Ships*, 46. See also Lepsius, *Denkmäler* II, pl. 28; Junker, *Gîza* 4, pl. 4; vol. 5, fig. 14b; Ziegler, *Akhethetep*, 66-67, 143. Depending on the size of the ship the number of steering oars is generally one to three, with rare examples of four or five (e.g., Lepsius, *Denkmäler* II, pl. 45a-b; Épron - Wild, *Ti* 1, pl. 49; Verner, *Ptahshepses*, photo 16, pl. 8).

223 When the deckhouse and awning do not extend to the extremity of the stern, the sailor handling the braces is usually shown standing on the deck at the stern behind the helmsmen. The figure sitting or kneeling on the cabin roof appeared in early in Dynasty 5 at Giza (e.g., Lepsius, *Denkmäler* II, pl. 22d; Junker, *Gîza* 2, fig. 22).

224 Vandier, *Manuel* 5, 697-98; Junker, *Gîza* 2, 66; Landström, *Ships*, 35-36; von Droste, *Der Igel*, 24-26. Other suggested identifications include the head of a ram or calf (Boreaux, *Nautique*, 277-78), a pig (Mackay et al., *Hemamieh*, 27), a lion (Jéquier, *BIFAO* 19 [1922], 50), a bird (Steindorff, *Catalogue Walters*, 78) or a goose (Kamal, *ASAE* 15 [1915], 218). Small boats carrying oils in the tomb of *Nj-ꜥnḫ-Ḫnmw* and *Ḫnmw-ḥtp* have figureheads of a hedgehog, hare, short-horned ox and long-horned ox (Moussa - Altenmüller, *Nianchchnum*, fig. 14, pl. 41), and a sailing boat with an animal head at both bow and stern is found in Upper Egypt in Dynasty 6 (Blackman, *Meir* 4, pl. 16). Animal heads on boats are attested in Egypt from predynastic times (see Berger, *Followers of Horus*, 107-20).

225 Compare Hassan, *Gîza* 5, fig. 114; Mogensen, *Mastaba egyptién*, fig. 13; Altenmüller, *Nianchchnum*, pl. 25, fig. 10; Hayes, *Scepter* 1, 100, fig. 56.

of them they are just starting to pull the oars through the water. In each boat a signalman stands among the rowers, facing the bow in the first and the stern in the second. Standing with legs apart and arms outstretched, he holds in his right hand a baton, which in the case of boats being rowed may be related to regulating the stroke when oars are in use. The two helmsmen stand, like those on the sailing ships, at the stern under the awning and guide the boat with long-handled oars. In the first of these boats, between the deckhouse and the helmsmen at the stern, is depicted a crew member leaning over the side of the boat and holding an object which is poorly preserved.

Two cargo boats in the bottom register face north like the sailing boats. The details are not well-preserved, but by comparison with the boats of the upper three registers, the wooden hulls are somewhat shorter and the bows and sterns thicker and slightly rounded.[226] The decks are almost completely covered by two cabins. Lookouts stand in the prow, two in the lead boat, with the first holding a staff or sounding pole, and one in the second. From the remaining lines they appear to wear the same belt with three flaps of cloth as do the crews on the ships in the registers above. Each boat is guided by two helmsmen with steering oars at the stern, one in the lead boat standing and the others kneeling on the rear cabin. Their mode of dress cannot be distinguished.

Each cargo boat is largely occupied by a rectangular-shaped deckhouse, and behind it a small cabin which arcs from the deck at the stern to slightly above the height of the deckhouse. Both appear to consist of a reinforced wooden frame enclosed with wickerwork.[227] The top and sides of each deckhouse are bound with a zig-zag lashing, like the posts of the deckhouses in the upper registers, and fragments of the same lashing are preserved on the frames of the small doors in the side.[228] Details of the freight carried in the first boat have largely disappeared, but above the deckhouse in the second can be seen what appear to be jars, loose grain and wrapped bundles of, probably, linen.

Colour

The wooden hulls of the passenger boats in top three registers are yellow outlined in orange-red, with dark red lashing on the papyriform boat in register 1. The prow and stern elements of the animal-headed boat in register 3 are bright blue with black outline; the animal's face yellow with black eye and outlined in red.[229] Sailing ships: bulwark dark red; bi-pod mast, stays, shrouds and rope braces black; top and bottom yard yellow with black line detail and outline, sail white with dark red outline. Deckhouse: awning white, red outline; upright supports white, lashing and outline black; woven matting black and yellow checks in the upper part (8 rows boats under sail, 10 rows boats under oar) above horizontal bands (3-6) of the

---

226 Examples and brief commentary are given by Landström, *Ships*, 60-61.

227 Vandier, *Manuel* 5, 751-55.

228 Similar detail is preserved in the tombs of *Rʿ-špss* (Lepsius, *Denkmäler* II, pl. 62) and *Snfrw-jn-jšt.f* (de Morgan, *Dahchour* 2, pl. 20).

229 The prow and stern elements are blue in the tombs of *Ftk.tj* (Boreaux, *Nautique*, 227 n.6 = Lepsius, *Denkmäler* II, pl. 96) and *Nj-ʿnḫ-H̱nmw* and *H̱nmw-ḥtp*, the last also retaining yellow on the face of the animal (personal observation).

same two colours in the lower part.[230] Length of similar matting hangs from roof at stern of sailing boats, and both aft and stern of boats under oar. Steering oars yellow with blade detail and outline orange-red; safety straps along shaft from oarlock to butt of blade black. Rowing oars dark red, some secured by black rowlocks. Staff held by tomb owner red except last boat in register 2 where it is black (paint only). Forked sounding pole and cord in hand black; *ḫrp* sceptre no colour. Object held over side by crewman yellow with orange-red outline (paint only). Cargo boats: hull dark red; wicker cabins yellow with narrow orange-red lines; horizontal support of main deckhouse black, upright posts, roof and door frame white with black lashing, door yellow. Sounding pole black; steering oar red. Cargo: bundles of linen white with red detail; grain yellow ground with orange-red detail; jars(?) dark red.

Commentary

The height of the registers has resulted in disproportionate sizes of the figures and the cabin in relation to the mast and of the mast to the hull. In the Old Kingdom, the height of the mast in proportion to the hull length averaged approximately 60%,[231] while those depicted here have a ratio of 38-43%. Similarly the length of the upper yard is normally between 1/3-2/3 of the mast height,[232] but here represented at 68-84%. A reduction of the usually larger figure of the tomb owner to fit a particular space as a participant in a scene is most common in boat scenes.[233] In the upper three registers the tomb owner is depicted approximately the same size as the helmsmen and signalmen who, like him, stand under the awning, and also the kilted figure facing him who does not. The owner is, however, considerably smaller than the lookouts standing at the bow of all boats. The head of the crewman seated on the deckhouse roof of the sailing ships reaches to the height of the mast and upper yard in all four examples.

Jrw-kȝ-Ptḥ is portrayed three times leaning on his staff, the usual mode of representing the tomb owner on boats, and three times holding the staff in front of him, a posture seldom encountered unless the tomb owner is seated.[234] Other rare

---

230 Where preserved, dark and light chequerboard squares above alternately dark and light horizontal bands is the standard pattern on the cabin enclosure (Vandier, *Manuel* 5, 788). Where recorded yellow and black are the most common colours e.g., Junker, *Gîza* 4, pls. 2-4, 7; Borchardt, *Denkmäler* 2, 190, 193, pls. 102, 104 = CG 1770, 1773; Moussa - Altenmüller, *Nefer*, pls. 16-17; idem, *Nianchchnum*, figs. 9-11, pls. 22, 25, 30; Kanawati, *A Mountain Speaks*, 68.

231 Vandier, *Manuel* 5, 798. Boreaux gives an increase in the proportional height from 50%-60% in Dynasty 4 to as much as 75% in Dynasty 5 (*Nautique*, 349).

232 Ibid, 365.

233 Smith, *HESPOK*, 300. For a discussion of a number of scenes in which the tomb owner is not depicted larger in size than the other figures, with examples from Memphite cemeteries dated from mid-Dynasty 5 to early Dynasty 6, see Vasiljević, *SAK* 25 [1998], 341-51. Note that she dates *Jj-nfrt* at Giza to Merenre-Pepy II (ibid, 343), presumably following Harpur (*Decoration*, 265) rather than Schürmann's placement in the second half of Dynasty 5 (*Ii-nefert*, 14), which I believe to be correct.

234 See Vandier, *Manuel* 5, 730, 863-65. For example, Lepsius, *Denkmäler* II, pl. 28; Junker, *Gîza* 4, pl. 5; vol. 6, fig. 16; Simpson, *Western Cemetery*, fig. 41; Mogensen, *Mastaba egyptién*, fig. 113; Duell, *Mereruka*, pls. 142-144; Altenmüller, *Mehu*, pl. 20; Davies, *Deir el-Gebrâwi* 2, pl. 19.

instances of a tomb owner standing in a boat with the staff held in front of him are attested in cemeteries at Memphis and in Upper Egypt. The pose occurs in the second half of Dynasty 5 in the tombs of *Ptḥ-špss* at Abusir and of *Nj-ʿnḫ-Ḫnmw* and *Ḫnmw-ḥtp* and of *Pḥ.n-wj-kꜣ.j* at Saqqara.[235] In Dynasty 6 an example appears in the Teti Cemetery and several others are found in Upper Egypt.[236]

The four registers in *Jrw-kꜣ-Ptḥ*'s tomb depicting ships powered by both sail and oar are a reflection of the importance of boats to life on the Nile, from the prehistoric periods and throughout Egyptian history. Old Kingdom wall scenes with various types of transport and cargo boats are most prevalent in the Memphite cemeteries between early Dynasty 5 and early Dynasty 6. Large travelling ships under oar and sail are depicted at Giza from the beginning of Dynasty 5, often placed at the entrance of the tomb or inside above the door.[237] Numerous and different types of travelling ships, under sail and oar, sometimes with cargo boats and occupying one or more registers on the same interior wall, appear in expanded decorative schemes from mid-Dynasty 5.[238] While four superposed registers filled with boats are seldom encountered, this feature is attested in the tombs of *Ptḥ-ḥtp* and *Ṯjj*,[239] near contemporaries at Saqqara of *Jrw-kꜣ-Ptḥ*.

The ships illustrated in *Jrw-kꜣ-Ptḥ*'s tomb include rather rare types of a papyriform boat and of a boat with an animal head at the prow. Papyriform boats in wood, quite commonly represented in the Old Kingdom and often found in religious contexts, are usually rowed or paddled and infrequently depicted under sail.[240] In addition to that of *Jrw-kꜣ-Ptḥ*, a papyriform boat with a sail is documented in the tombs of *Ṯjj* at Saqqara and of *Jntj* at Deshasha,[241] both dated to the end of Dynasty 5. A few other examples occur in Dynasty 6, one at Giza and possibly three in Upper Egypt.[242] The hedgehog figurehead is found on sailboats, cargo boats and on smaller boats used for pleasure trips or hunting in the marshes, but seldom on a travelling ship being rowed which shows neither stepped mast nor sails.[243] Examples are found at Giza between late Dynasty 4 and early

---

235 Respectively, Verner, *Ptahshepses*, photo 16, pl. 8; Moussa - Altenmüller, *Nianchchnum*, figs. 9, 11, pls. 22, 30; Lepsius, *Denkmäler* II, pl. 45b.

236 Kanawati - Abder-Raziq, *Teti Cemetery* 5, pls. 28, 56; Blackman, *Meir* 4, pl. 16; Kanawati, *El-Hawawish* 2, fig. 19; vol. 4, fig. 17; vol. 7, fig. 30; vol. 8, fig. 12.

237 E.g., Lepsius, *Denkmäler* II, pls. 22, 28; Junker, *Gîza* 2, fig. 22; Weeks, *Cemetery G 6000,* fig. 25. For examples at Memphis later in Dynasty 5 see Lepsius, *Denkmäler* II, pls. 45, 64bis. In Upper Egypt ships under sail or oar also appear early in Dynasty 5 (El-Khouli - Kanawati, *El-Hammamiya*, pls. 35, 37, 44-45) and a few others are attested at the end of that dynasty, but the large majority date to Dynasty 6. Harpur suggests that this theme was inspired by royal reliefs of early Dynasty 5 (*Decoration*, 56).

238 For example Borchardt, *Denkmäler* 1, pls. 50, 102, 104 = CG 1536, 1769, 1770, 1773; Mogensen, *Mastaba egyptién*, pls. 5-6; Verner, *Ptahshepses*, photos 9-13, 16, pls. 3-5, 9; Moussa - Junge, *Two Craftsmen*, pl. 8.

239 Respectively, Lepsius, *Denkmäler* II, pls. 103b, 104b; Épron - Wild, *Ti* 1, pls. 22, 24, 26, 47-49. Early in Dynasty 6 a large number of boats are placed together in one (Altenmüller, *Mehu*, pls. 19-21) or two (Duell, *Mereruka*, pls. 140-45) long registers.

240 See Vandier, *Manuel* 5, 691-96, 780; Landström, *Ships*, 56-57; Jones, *Boats*, 43-44.

241 Respectively, Épron - Wild, *Ti* 1, pl. 47; Kanawati - McFarlane, *Deshasha*, pl. 32.

242 Junker, *Gîza* 4, pls. 5, 7; Petrie, *Deshasheh*, pl. 27; Davies, *Deir el-Gebrâwi* 2, pl. 19; perhaps de Morgan, *Catalogue des monuments* 1, 160.

243 See Vandier, *Manuel* 5, 697-98, 780; von Droste, *Der Igel*, 93-117.

Dynasty 5 in the tombs of *Mr.s-ꜥnḫ* III, *Sšꜣt-ḥtp* and *Nswt-nfr*,[244] and at Saqqara in the second half of Dynasty 5 in the tombs of *Nj-ꜥnḫ-Ḫnmw* and *Ḫnmw-ḥtp*, *Ṯjj*, *Rꜥ-m-kꜣ.j* in the Metropolitan Museum and probably also on a fragment now in Baltimore.[245] Only those of *Mr.s-ꜥnḫ*, *Nj-ꜥnḫ-Ḫnmw* and *Ṯjj* depict the boat being propelled, like that of *Jrw-kꜣ-Ptḥ*, by oars rather than paddles.

The motif of a crewman leaning over the side of a boat is not common but there are several parallels at Saqqara and Abusir all dated in the period Neuserre-Djedkare. A boat under sail in the tomb of *Ꜣḫt-ḥtp* shows a man, similarly near the helmsmen, who leans far over the ship's side to dip a wide-mouthed bowl into the water; adjacent to him, seated under the deckhouse awning, is a man holding a bird.[246] On another sailboat in the nearby tomb of *Nfr* and *Kꜣ.j-ḥꜣ.j* a man, positioned about the middle of the cabin, is lowering into the water on a rope a large, ovoid shaped object.[247] A cargo boat in the tomb of *Ptḥ-špss* at Abusir shows a man amidships, near the cabin door, pouring water from a jar over the rail, and on another cargo boat in the mastaba of *Ḥtp-ḥr-ꜣḫtj* from Saqqara a similarly shaped object is being lowered to the water on a rope held by a man kneeling at the stern.[248] The objects depicted in *Nfr* and *Kꜣ.j-ḥꜣ.j* and in *Ḥtp-ḥr-ꜣḫtj* could be fenders, but are unlikely to be anchors. It may be questionable whether any anchor, presumably of stone, is represented on these transport vessels of the Old Kingdom.[249] The yellow paint preserved on the hull of *Jrw-kꜣ-Ptḥ*'s boat does not appear to have the shape of a jar, fender or anchor, but its faded outline resembles that of the bird(?) dangled over the side of a sailboat by a man standing amidships in the Saqqara tomb of *Ḫnmw-ḥtp*.[250]

Inscriptions

Pls. 3b, 41-42, 44-45, 47-49

The tomb has few inscriptions, the only text in a wall scene being the name and title of the tomb owner painted before his seated figure at the north end of the east wall (see above). A single horizontal line of text is inscribed across the east and

244 Respectively, Dunham - Simpson, *Mersyankh III*, fig. 5; Junker, *Gîza* 2, fig. 32; vol. 3, fig. 29.

245 Respectively, Moussa - Altenmüller, *Nianchchnum*, pl. 30, fig. 11; Épron - Wild, *Ti* 1, pl. 49; Hayes, *Scepter* 1, fig. 56; Steindorff, *Catalogue Walters*, 78, pl. 50.

246 Ziegler, *Akhethetep*, 66-67. As well as this bird held by a seated crew member, in the tomb of *Mḥw* a boat, mast stepped and under oar, is followed by a small skiff in which is depicted a man offering birds to the tomb owner seated at the stern (Altenmüller, *Mehu*, pl. 20a). Elsewhere, a man standing in the stern of a boat under oar with a stepped mast offers a bird to a large standing figure of *Mrrw-kꜣ.j* (Duell, *Mereruka*, pl. 145).

247 Moussa - Altenmüller, *Nefer*, 26, pl. 16.

248 Respectively, Verner, *Ptahshepses*, 15, photo 12, pl. 5; Mohr, *Hetep-her-akhti*, fig. 17. Note that in each of these tombs a man on a nearby cargo ship is shown drinking from a similar jar (Verner, *Ptahshepses*, photo 11, pl. 3; Mohr, *Hetep-her-akhti*, fig. 18).

249 None is illustrated at or near the bow where an anchor is normally deployed, although one could have been attached to the end of a coiled rope played out over the bow of a sailing ship in the Sixth Dynasty tomb of *Ḏꜥw* at Deir el-Gebrawi (Davies, *Deir el-Gebrâwi* 2, pl. 7). For different opinions refer to Boreaux, *Nautique*, 414-17; Jéquier, *BIFAO* 19 [1922], 128-29; Jones, *Boats*, 69.

250 Petrie - Murray, *Memphite Chapels*, 26, pl. 17:6.

north walls, beneath the scenes and above the statues, the signs incised and painted in polychrome colours. The text begins at the south end of the east wall, above the statues drafted in red and the registers of boats (1), is interrupted by the panel of marsh scenes and continues above the first statue niche (2), concluding over the statues on the north wall (3).

(1) *ḥtp dj nswt Jnpw ḫntj zḥ-nṯr nb tꜣ ḏsr tpj ḏw.f jmj wt ḫp.f nfr ḥr wꜣwt nfr(w)t ḫppt jmꜣḫ(w) [ḥr.sn]*[251] (2) *ḥtp dj nswt Jnpw tpj ḏw.f jmj wt nb t3 ḏsr ḥtp dj Wsjr nb Ḏdw*[252] *ḫntj zḥ-nṯr*[253] *qrs.tj.f*[254] *m ḫrt-nṯr m zmjt jmntjt jꜣw nfr jmꜣḫ(w) ḫr nṯr ꜥꜣ* (3) *qbḥ nmt pr-ꜥꜣ Jrw-kꜣ-Ptḥ* '(1) An offering which the king gives and Anubis foremost of the divine booth, lord of the sacred land, who is on his hill, who is in the embalming place (gives), that he may travel well on the beautiful roads upon which the honoured (ones) travel. (2) An offering which the king gives and which Anubis, who is on his hill, who is in the embalming place, lord of the sacred land (gives); an offering which Osiris, Lord of Busiris, foremost of the divine booth gives, that he be buried in the necropolis in the western desert having reached a good old age, the honoured one before the great god, (3) the libationer and butcher of the palace, Irukaptah'.

Beneath this text, a line of vertical inscriptions with the titles and name of the tomb owner is incised on six of the seven piers separating the statue niches on the east wall. No inscriptions are found on the pier between the two statues on the north wall but traces of black paint at the top are possibly part of the sign , suggesting that an inscription was drafted but not completed. The vertical texts on the east wall are not oriented in the same direction, but face each other in groups of two,[255] and in each line the signs are painted either black or blue. Inscriptions 1 and 2, both black, face statue number 3; lines 3 painted blue and 4 painted black face statue number 5; and lines 5 in black and 6 in blue face statue number 7.

The lines read, from the south:
1) *qbḥ nmt pr-ꜥꜣ jmꜣḫ(w)*[256] *ḫr nṯr ꜥꜣ nmt ꜥbw-r nswt rḫ nswt Jr[w-kꜣ]-Ptḥ* 'the libationer and butcher of the palace, the honoured one before the great god, the butcher of the king's repast, the acquaintance of the king, Irukaptah'.
2) *qbḥ nmt ꜥbw-r*[257] *nswt jmꜣḫ(w) ḫr nṯr ꜥꜣ wꜥb nswt rḫ nswt [Jrw-kꜣ-Ptḥ]* 'the libationer and butcher of the king's repast, the honoured one before the great god, the *wꜥb*-priest of the king, the acquaintance of the king, Irukaptah'.

---

251 The signs are here arranged . For the usual form and completion of this phrase see Lapp, *Opferformel*, 53.

252 The is omitted in the writing of *Ḏdw*.

253 Associated with Anubis and his most common epithet in Dynasty 5, there is no evidence that *ḫntj zḥ-nṯr* was attributed to Osiris (Barta, *Opferliste*, 8, 15, 25, 232-33; Begelsbacher-Fischer, *Götterwelt des Alten Reiches*, 29-30, 121-125). Its use here as an epithet for Osiris is remarkable.

254 The two groups of signs in *qrs* are transposed, resulting in rather than .

255 A rare example of inscriptions on piers of individual statue niches is preserved in the tomb of *Jdw* at Giza; there, the texts on each of the four piers and the horizontal inscription above all face the same direction (Simpson, *Qar and Idu*, fig. 36).

256 The word is consistently written without the *w* in all inscriptions.

257 This group of signs is written which differs from the writing of the title *rḫ nswt* before the name at the end of this column. No other title sequence on the piers starts with

3) *qbḥ nmt pr-ꜥꜣ rḫ nswt jmꜣḫ(w) ḫr nṯr ꜥꜣ wꜥb nswt Jrw-[kꜣ]-Ptḥ* 'the libationer and butcher of the palace, the acquaintance of the king, the honoured one before the great god, the *wꜥb*-priest of the king, Irukaptah'.
4) *qbḥ nmt ꜥbw-r nswt jmꜣḫ(w) ḫr nṯr ꜥꜣ wꜥb nswt Jrw-[kꜣ]-Ptḥ* 'the libationer and butcher of the king's repast, the honoured one before the great god, the *wꜥb*-priest of the king, Irukaptah'.
5) *qbḥ nmt pr-ꜥꜣ jmꜣḫ(w) ḫr Ptḥ rsj*[258] *jnb.f nmt ꜥbw-r nswt [Jrw-kꜣ]-Ptḥ* 'the libationer and butcher of the palace, the honoured one before Ptah, south of his wall, the butcher of the king's repast, Irukaptah'.
6) *qbḥ ꜥbw-r nswt jmꜣḫ(w) ḫr Ptḥ rsj jnb.f wꜥb nswt [Jrw-kꜣ]-Ptḥ* 'the libationer of the king's repast, the honoured one before Ptah, south of his wall, the *wꜥb*-priest of the king, Irukaptah'.

West Wall

The decoration on the west wall includes no scenes and is limited to a false door and engaged statues.

THE FALSE DOOR

Pls. 22-23, 50

The false door is monolith of good quality limestone which has been set into the native rock towards the southern end of the west wall. The door has a cavetto cornice, torus moulding, one pair of jambs and is, with the exception of a text in black paint on the upper lintel, decorated in incised and painted relief. Some internal modelling is present on figures of the tomb owner, seated on the panel and standing on the jambs. At the bottom of each jamb is a dado, a feature which occurs nowhere else in this tomb.

The Upper Lintel: One line of inscription reads: *rḫ nswt jmꜣḫ(w) ḫr nṯr ꜥꜣ Ḫnw* 'the acquaintance of the king, the honoured one before the great god, Khenu'.

The Central Panel: Across the top of the central panel is a single horizontal line of text placed on a red guideline which reads: *qbḥ*[259] *nmt pr-ꜥꜣ rḫ nswt Jrw-kꜣ-Ptḥ* 'the libationer and butcher of the palace, the acquaintance of the king Irukaptah'. Two more red guidelines are preserved above the loaves on the offering table in an area showing small patches of pale green, perhaps suggesting additional decoration or text in the now empty space above the loaves. The tomb owner is depicted seated on a chair in front of an offering table with twelve half-loaves of bread. He wears a shoulder length wig, broad collar and plain kilt, with his left hand clenched against his chest and his open right hand extended palm down to the offering table. The chair on which he sits, with neither back nor cushion, has a papyrus umbel finial, a bull's leg and, like the two other chairs represented in the tomb, no visible

---

rḫ nswt. Considering that *qbḥ nmt* is normally (except on the left jamb of the false door) associated with *pr-ꜥꜣ* or *ꜥbw-r nswt*, it may be assumed that the intended word was 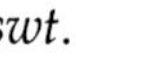. Note that the initial words inscribed on each pier alternate between *pr-ꜥꜣ* and *ꜥbw-r nswt*.

258 Note a reversal of the sign *rsj*.

259 The direction of the jar is reversed on the panel, lower lintel and left jamb.

front leg. Placed on a low table to the right of the offering table stand are a ewer and basin and a tall beer jar. To the left of the table stand is written: *ḫꜣ šs ḫꜣ mnḫt t ḥnqt pꜣt ꜣpd kꜣ* 'one thousand of alabaster, one thousand of clothes (and) bread, beer, cakes, fowl and oxen'.

The Lower Lintel: *rḫ nswt qbḥ nmt ꜥbw-r nswt*[260] *Ḫnw* 'the acquaintance of the king, the libationer and butcher of the king's repast, Khenu'.

Drum: *Jrw-kꜣ-Ptḥ* 'Irukaptah'.

The Right Jamb: Each of the jambs has two short vertical (1-2) and one horizontal (3) lines of texts, the last giving only the tomb owner's name. The hieroglyphs on the right jamb read: (1) *qbḥ nmt pr-ꜥꜣ* (2) *wꜥb nswt jmꜣḫ(w)* (3) *Jrw-kꜣ-Ptḥ* '(1) the libationer and butcher of the palace, (2) the *wꜥb*-priest of the king, the honoured one, (3) Irukaptah'. Beneath the name and occupying nearly half the jamb is a standing figure of the tomb owner who wears a short wig, collar and pointed kilt and holds in his right hand a staff and in his left a folded cloth. Standing in front of *Jrw-kꜣ-Ptḥ* and holding his staff is a very small unclothed male figure, designated by the text above him as *zꜣ.f Ptḥ-šps* 'his son, Ptahshepses'.

The Left Jamb: A similar arrangement of inscriptions on the left jamb reads: (1) *rḫ nswt qbḥ nmt*[261] (2) *jmꜣḫ(w) ḫr nṯr ꜥꜣ* (3) *Ḫnw* '(1) the acquaintance of the king, the libationer and butcher, (2) the honoured one before the great god, (3) Khenu'. The lower part of the jamb has a figure of the tomb owner which is virtually identical to that on the right jamb, except that he wears a shoulder-length wig. Also similarly represented is a small unclothed figure who is identified as *zꜣ.f smsw Ptḥ-špss* 'his eldest son, Ptahshepses'. As this figure is taller than that on the right jamb and is designated 'eldest son' it is likely that each figure represents a different son with the same name.

Colour

The false door is unfinished with no indication of cornice leaves, roughly cut apertures and guidelines still evident on the panel and dado. The central niche shows signs of red and black, painted in imitation of granite, and de Rachewiltz reported traces of green at the top which are no longer visible.[262] Remnants of red and black paint on the moulding may suggest preparation for lashing decoration on the torus. Beneath the decoration of the jambs is a dado, showing remains of red guidelines above a wide black band extending to the base of the jambs. The two bands are separated by a narrow black line, and the upper band of the right jamb retains traces of red paint. Some colours of the relief decoration are preserved, especially on the hieroglyphic signs although the text on the upper lintel is only drafted in black paint.

---

260 The conventional writing of *qbḥ nmt ꜥbw-r nswt* with honorific transposition is not followed, possibly because the string begins with *rḫ nswt*. The sequence on the central panel and on the east wall places *rḫ nswt* following *Jrw-kꜣ-Ptḥ*'s butchery titles.

261 As on the lower lintel, *rḫ nswt* precedes *qbḥ nmt* which here, perhaps because of lack of space, is written without an affiliation with the royal house.

262 *Irw-k3-Ptḥ*, 26.

Male flesh red, hair, brows and eye detail black, kilts white (no red outline). Staff yellow (no outline); folded cloth white. Chair black with yellow markings; offering table loaves yellow; ewer and basin traces of blue (no outline).

Commentary

The use of the cavetto cornice and torus moulding on a false door with only a single pair of jambs is very unusual. False doors are generally placed in two categories: those with no cornice, including palace façade type doors, and those with torus moulding and cavetto cornice.[263] The first type may have one or two pair of jambs, with or without a surrounding frame, while those with a cornice and moulding have two or three pairs of jambs.[264] The cavetto cornice, known from the early Old Kingdom and found as an architectural element in pyramid temples of early Dynasty 5, was incorporated into the false door in the first half of Dynasty 5 at Saqqara, becoming more common in the latter part of that dynasty.[265] The early examples at both Saqqara and Giza have two pairs of jambs.[266] Both types of doors, as well as a palace façade false door,[267] are found in the rock-cut tombs south of the Unis causeway. The two false doors of *Jrw-kꜣ-Ptḥ*'s neighbour *Ꜣḫt-ḥtp*, five in the tomb of *Nfr* and *Kꜣ.j-ḥꜣ.j* and four in that of *Nj-ꜥnḫ-H̱nmw* and *H̱mnw-ḥtp* have a single pair of jambs within a frame,[268] while the wives of *Nj-ꜥnḫ-H̱nmw* and *H̱mnw-ḥtp* have double jambs.[269] Three doors in the tombs of *Jrj.n-kꜣ-Ptḥ* and *Sḫntjw* and *Nfr-sšm-Ptḥ*, adjacent to *Nj-ꜥnḫ-H̱nmw* and *H̱mnw-ḥtp*, have a cavetto cornice and torus moulding with two pairs of jambs.[270] The cavetto cornice door of *Jrw-kꜣ-Ptḥ* having a single pair of jambs within a torus moulding is, to my knowledge, unattested elsewhere;[271] isolated examples found at Giza and Upper Egypt in Dynasty 6 lack a true torus moulding. A small unfinished door with one pair of jambs is incised for a woman at the southern end of a wall in the tomb of *Ṯtw*, which holds also five large cavetto cornice doors of the standard type.[272] Another example with only a suggestion of a torus moulding

---

263 Rusch, *ZÄS* 58 [1923], 101-24; Vandier, *Manuel* 2, 394-408; Wiebach, *Scheintür*, 8-10; Strudwick, *Administration*, 15-17.

264 Rusch, *ZÄS* 58 [1923], 120 (Pl. A), 122 (Pl. B).

265 Ibid, 113; Reisner, *Giza*, 378-79; Vandier, *Manuel* 2, 401-403; Wiebach, *Scheintür*, 128-35; Cherpion, *Mastabas et hypogées*, 75, 197-98: Criterion 54. According to Strudwick (*Administration*, 15) the earliest example is in the tomb of *Pr-sn* (Petrie - Murray, *Memphite Chapels*, pl. 19).

266 E.g., Lepsius, *Denkmäler* II, pl. 48; Murray, *Saqqara* 1, pls. 8, 20, 32; Épron - Wild, *Ti* 3, pls. 182-85; Hassan, *Gîza* 6:3, 24, pl. 9B.

267 Moussa - Altenmüller, *Nefer*, pls. 28, 31.

268 Respectively, Badawi, *ASAE* 40 [1941], pl. 47; Moussa - Altenmüller, *Nefer*, pls. 29, 32, 36, 39; idem, *Nianchchnum*, pls. 80a, 92, fig. 26.

269 Moussa - Altenmüller, *Nianchchnum*, pl. 81a.

270 Moussa - Junge, *Two Craftsmen*, fig. 1, ills, 1-3. While other false doors in the Unis causeway are of limestone, that of *Jrj.n-kꜣ-Ptḥ* (ibid, ill. 3) is rock cut with painted decoration on plaster.

271 Cavetto cornice doors with single jambs are not mentioned in Rusch (*ZÄS* 58 [1923], 101-124), Vandier (*Manuel* 2, 401-410), Wiebach (*Scheintür*, 128-53) or Strudwick (*Administration*, 9-52).

272 Simpson, *Western Cemetery*, figs. 10, 15, pl. 27C (G2001).

is preserved at El-Hawawish in Upper Egypt, painted on a plastered rock surface in the tomb of *Sfḫw*.[273]

Also unusual are the twelve half-loaves on the offering table on the false door panel depicted as five pairs facing each other and a single half loaf at each end facing outward. This feature also occurs on the panel of *Ḫmnw-ḥtp*'s false door in the nearby tomb he shares with his brother, *Nj-ʿnḫ-Ḫnmw*,[274] although elsewhere in the tomb loaves on the offering tables are depicted in the more common orientations of each half facing inward or all loaves as pairs (with stems).[275]

V THE STATUES

The tomb has 14 niches cut into three of the walls, two on the north, eight on the east and four on the west, each holding a single engaged rock-cut statue. It is also apparent that the original decorative program planned for two additional statues on the east wall and another three on the west wall. The statues in the north and east walls occupy the lower two-thirds of both walls, beneath the painted relief scenes in the upper part, while those in the west occupy the full wall height. A comparison of photographs from 1940 showing the original condition with others taken in 1957,[276] gives some indication of the damage suffered by these statues in the two decades following the tomb's discovery. Although a few painted details have since disappeared, conservation measures carried out in recent years by the Department of Restoration at Saqqara has ensured stability of the tomb's decoration.

East Wall, south

Pls. 19, 47

Between the boating scenes and the serdab are partially preserved the painted red outlines of two frontal figures.[277] They have the same size and stance as do the ten male statues carved in the east and north walls and were obviously drafted as the first step in the production of two more engaged statues. Three heads, overlapping lines and a surfeit of vertical lines for niches indicate some uncertainty or difficulty in their placement. Of the southernmost figure all that remains are the head and shoulders, beneath which the wall has been repaired in modern times. Several

---

273 Kanawati, *El-Hawawish* 6, fig. 11.

274 Moussa - Altenmüller, *Nianchchnum*, fig. 26, pl. 92. Presumably the adjacent damaged false door of *Nj-ʿnḫ-Ḫnmw* received the same decoration.

275 Ibid, figs. 20, 25, pls. 87, 88. For other paired loaves see e.g., Mariette, *Mastabas*, 247; Murray, *Saqqara* 1, pl. 27; Hassan, *Gîza* 2, 112, 115.

276 De Rachewiltz, *Irw-k3-Ptḥ*, pls. 4-5, 8-11. See also this volume *Pl. 27*.

277 Similar outlines in red of three frontal figures within a niche frame are preserved in the tomb of *Nfr-ḥr-n-Ptḥ* (Abu-Bakr, *Giza*, 121-22, fig. 98, pl. 67A). Guidelines for two figures are reported in the tomb of *Sḫm-kȝ-Rʿ* (Hassan, *Gîza* 4, 106). Compare the low relief frontal figure in the central niche of the false door of *Rdj-n.s* (Smith, *HESPOK*, pl. 57c, from G5032 now in Boston).

overlapping lines indicate corrections, perhaps to better centre it in a niche. Adjacent to the north is a head and part of the shoulders, the sketch probably abandoned upon realising that no room had been allowed for a pier. The right side of the wig is overlapped by that of a more complete figure to the north. Preserved are the lines of the head, wig, eyes, torso, breasts, right arm with the hand grasping a cloth, right side of the kilt and its belt tab, part of the right leg and a vertical guideline running through the sternum to the kilt. Other vertical lines presumably are guidelines for niches. Two of these pass through the figures in the wrong places, suggesting that the placement of a pier between the statues may have been overlooked in the original design, requiring an alteration to reposition both the niches and the figures. The long line passing from head to knee of the northernmost figure was evidently a first attempt to outline the niche, with the corrected line, partially preserved, placed north of the head. The two central vertical lines, one passing through the unfinished head, define a pier between two niches with resulting measurements which approximate the average width of the niches (.44m.) and piers (.14m.) of the finished statues on this wall.

East Wall, north; North Wall

Pls. 4, 24-30, 36a, 41

Directly north of the panel with marsh scenes and beneath the horizontal line of text is the first of eight individual statue niches which extend to the end of the east wall and continue, like the *ḥtp dj nswt* formula above them, on the north wall with an additional two niches. As the engaged statues on the east and north walls are so similar, they will be treated as one unit (Nos. 1-10) in the description which follows. The niches cut into both walls have a sill height .25m. above the floor and average dimensions of .44m. wide x 1.35m. high. Their depth is greater in the area surrounding the feet (sill) than at the head (ceiling) and shallower yet in the area between the arms and torso. The walls, ceilings and floors of these niches were roughly finished, coated with plaster and painted a clear mid-blue-grey, now only partially preserved. The niches are separated by piers .14m. wide which in recent times have been restored in the lower part to an average height of .40m. Those which are better preserved show a plastered ground painted mid-grey, and all but the southernmost pier on the east wall are decorated with carved and painted vertical inscriptions with the titles and name *Jrw-kꜣ-Ptḥ*. The pier between the two statues on the north wall appears to lack decoration but a trace of black paint at the top suggests that inscriptions may have been drafted.

GENERAL DESCRIPTION

Nine of the ten niches each hold a standing figure of *Jrw-kꜣ-Ptḥ* carved in high relief in the rock, then smoothed, coated with a creamy plaster and painted. The statue in the southernmost niche along the east wall was never completed. All the figures stand in a rigid, erect posture with both feet together and both arms hanging beside the body, clenched fists holding a rolled or folded cloth. They wear short rounded wigs which cover the ear but do not touch the shoulder, broad collars and kilts. The face is squarish, the eyebrows curved, the eyes round with pointed canthi, the nose straight and broad with rounded tip, the mouth horizontal with thick upper and lower lips and rounded chin. Naso-labial creases and a philtrum above the upper lip are distinct on Nos. 3, 5, 10. The shoulders are broad with no clavicle definition and the torso, with slight indications of breasts and a vertical abdominal muscle above a shallow navel, tapers to a slender waist. The arms are generally tubular with some suggestion of biceps and forearm musculature and the thumbnail is rounded. The legs are tubular with knees and shin bones indicated, and toes of the feet, most complete on Nos. 7, 8, 10, slightly splayed. The condition of the statues is relatively good, retaining a fair portion of the original paint, but none are fully preserved and all have received some repair in modern times.

Although similar in size, appearance and decoration, the statues are not exactly the same in their measurements and there are variations in body proportions. The averages are given here, with exceptions in parentheses:

Top of wig to chin .16-.18m. (No. 2=.195m., No. 7=.19m.)
Shoulder width .37-.41m. (No. 10=.35m.)
Chest width .24-.27m. (Nos. 2, 10=.20m.)
Waist width .16-.19m. (No. 2=.145m., No. 10=.15m.)
Arm length from shoulder to clenched fist .53-.60m. (No. 2=.49m.)
Top of collar to top of belt .28-.33m.
Kilt length .32-.37m. (No. 10=.40m.)
Hem of kilt to soles of feet .46-.49m. (No. 2=.45m., No. 9=.42m., No. 10=.43m.).

The colour remaining on the statues will be noted in the individual descriptions which follow, but a few general comments may be made. The negative spaces between the arms and the torso as well as between the legs are painted the same mid-blue-grey as the niche walls and piers. The flesh of all statues is strong brown-red, faded on virtually all feet. Hair, eyebrows and eye outlines are black, with red detail on the eyeballs of Nos. 2, 5 and 7 and a dark red brown iris on No. 3. Moustaches preserved on Nos. 2 and 3 (also originally on No. 4) and nipples on Nos. 2, 4, 5 and 6 are painted black. Thumbnails and folded cloths held in hands are white. Collars are primarily blue, green and white with black outline; the blue and green are now faded, but tiny fragments of the original strong, cobalt blue are visible on Nos. 6 and 8. Plain kilts with a knotted belt are white with red outline (Nos. 3 and 6); more elaborate kilts are half white and half yellow with an intricate belt, buckle and ties (Nos. 5 and 8), three with the addition of hanging strands of beads (Nos. 2, 4 and 7).

STATUE 1

Pls. 4a, 24-25

Niche H = 1.35m.; W = .45m.; D = sill .13m.(S) and .10m.(N), ceiling .09m.
Statue H = 1.34m.

A single statue of a male, resembling others on the east and north walls, is unfinished, the background cut away around the head and legs but the figure itself on the same plane with no modelling. The figure retains a coarse outline in black paint, averaging .01m. in thickness, around the head and body, including eye, collar, breast and kilt. The paint is also visible at the bottom of the wig, the roughly cut separation of the arms and torso, and the upper part of the legs, all areas where background cutting had begun. It is probable that the original outline was executed not in black but, as preserved on the uncut figures drafted on the east and west walls, in red paint. This undoubtedly disappeared in the course of chiselling to rough out the figure and a new guide for the sculptors drawn in black. The right side of the face, right shoulder, left lower arm and both legs below the knees, as well as the sill have in recent times been repaired in plaster.[278]

It is possible that this statue was not part of the original design program, but a later addition. Among all the statues in niches on the east and north walls, this is the only one not finished in high relief, smoothed, plastered and painted in detail. Vertical inscriptions were incised and painted on all piers between the niches of the east wall except for that between statues No. 1 and No. 2, which shows no evidence of even a drafted text. Above No. 2 is the unfinished frame of a cavetto cornice like that over the southernmost statue niche of the west wall. Perhaps the initial intent was that the east wall, like the west wall, have seven statues, but after their completion an eighth was added. Note that some of the marsh activities depicted adjacent to the unfinished statue do not appear to fit well in the space available to the south of its niche.

STATUE 2

Pls. 4a, 24-25

Niche H = 1.35m.(S) and 1.34m.(N); W = .43m.; D = sill and ceiling .10m.
Statue H = 1.33m.

Above this statue niche faint red lines found in the band of horizontal inscription define a painted and partly carved outline of a cavetto cornice frame similar to those designed for the statue niches on the west wall. The statue is in good condition with slight damage to nose and mouth, and repair on the left arm above the elbow and diagonally across the upper part of the kilt. The head, .195m. from top of wig to chin, is larger than the average and appears to be outsized for the body proportions, yet does not reach the top of the niche.

Colour

Hair, brows, moustache and nipples black. Eye outline and pupil black, eyeballs white with orange-red shading. A well-preserved collar has, like Nos. 3 and 7, seven bands: top row of small rectangles alternately light green and light blue, a narrow band of white, three broad bands of light blue, light green and light blue interspersed with vertical spacers of blue edged on either side by two narrow bands of white and blue, then another narrow white band and the bottom row like the top. Left thumbnail and folded cloth white. Kilt clear ochre yellow on right side and white on left with details well-preserved. Belt formed of rectangular blocks of light green alternating with narrower blocks of white edged on either side in light blue with a black vertical zig-zag pattern; upper and lower belt edges patterned with

---

278 For a view of the original state in which this statue was found see de Rachewiltz, *Irw-k3-Ptḥ*, pls. 4-5, 7:2.

narrow rectangular blocks alternately light blue and white, buckle fastening blue; all outlines black.[279] Belt tab yellow with horizontal red lines, edged in light blue, outlined on both sides in black; ties red with two bands at ends showing traces of light green. Four strands of beads hanging from belt to hem of kilt composed of lozenge-shaped beads of red and light green separated by round blue beads, the blue and green beads outlined in black, and ending in yellow tassels outlined in red.[280]

STATUE 3

Pls. 4, 24, 26-27, 36a

Niche H = 1.33m.; W = sill .42m., ceiling .44m.; D = sill .16m., ceiling .10m.(S) and .13m.(N)
Statue H = 1.33m.

Modern repair exists on upper chest, right leg below knee, left knee and shin. Both feet are gone. Plaster has fallen from the nose but the face is otherwise well-preserved.

Colour

Hair, brows, moustache black. Eye outine black, dark brown-red pupil, white eyeballs. Thumbnails and folded cloth white. Plain kilt and knotted belt white with red detail and outline. Collar with seven bands and spacers, similar to that of No. 2, was originally more complete.[281]

STATUE 4

Pls. 4, 24, 26-27

Niche H = 1.34m.; W = .45m.; D = sill .20m., ceiling .13m.
Statue H = 1.34m.

At the time of discovery this was probably the finest and best preserved of all the statues, but the face was removed even before de Rachewiltz published his report.[282] All that remains of the head is part of the wig, but earlier photographs show the complete face, including a moustache. Both damaged shoulders have been repaired as well as small sections in the lower part of the legs above the ankles.

---

279 Similar patterning and colouring of the kilt, belt, buckle and tab is recorded for the double statue of *Nj-mꜣꜥt-sd* (Borchardt, *Statuen* 1, 100 = CG 133).

280 Beads and tassels of the same colours can be seen on the statue of *3ḫt-ḥtp* in the Egyptian Museum (JdE 93164) and are reported by Borchardt, *Statuen* 1, 53, 170 (CG 60, 268) and Kaplony, *Methethi*, 61 (Brooklyn 50.77). On another statue of *Mṯtj* (Brooklyn 53.222) the beads are green, red and black (ibid, 66).

281 For a view before some of the painted plaster fell see de Rachewiltz, *Irw-k3-Ptḥ*, 9, pl. 5.

282 Ibid, 9, compare pls. 4-5 with pls. 8:2, 9:2. See also this volume *Pl. 27.*

Colour

Paint well-preserved on body, necklace and kilt. Hair and nipples black. Broad collar of nine bands, all outlined in black: top and bottom rows composed of narrow rectangles alternating light blue and white; between are seven bands: narrow white, broad bands of blue, light green, blue, light green, blue, narrow white (differs from No. 2). Unusual painted black lines on the chest beneath and following the rounded line of the collar and then v-shaped down either side of the median chest line towards the kilt. Thumbnails and folded cloth white. Kilt clear yellow on right side and white on left with elaborate belt, buckle, ties and four strands of hanging beads, almost identical to No. 2.

STATUE 5

Pls. 4a, 24, 28

Niche H = 1.33m.(S) and 1.34m.(N); W = .435-.44m.; D = sill .15m., ceiling .10m.
Statue H = 1.32m.

The statue has a vertical repair extending from the chin and neck down the centre of the chest and including part of the kilt, but is otherwise well-preserved. The break resulted from a fracture or weakness in the rock which can also be seen in the upper part of the wall, running through the figure of the last offering bearer.[283] The face of the statue is complete other than slight damage to the nose. The right eye is noticeably lower than the left and angled slightly downward.

Colour

Hair, brows, eye outline and pupil black, orange-red shading on eyeballs. Collar damaged and retains traces only of blue, white and of black outline, but appears similar to Nos. 3 and 7. Nipples black, thumbnail of right hand white. Little paint remains on damaged kilt, reported as yellow and white,[284] and fallen plaster has, presumably, exposed a painted red line down left side of kilt. Poorly preserved belt detail, parts of belt tab and of red ties resemble No. 8.

STATUE 6

Pls. 24, 28

Niche H = 1.34m. (sides) and 1.37m. (centre); W = .43m.; D = sill .165m., ceiling .10m.
Statue H = 1.37m.

De Rachewiltz reported the face already missing at the time of discovery,[285] only the eyebrows remaining, but the rest of the statue is well-preserved. The wig is longer than that of other statues, being .02m. above the shoulder against the average .04m.

---

283 Ibid, 10, pls. 10:1, 19:2.
284 Ibid, 10.
285 Ibid, 10, pl. 4.

Colour

Hair, brows, nipples black. Brown-red flesh colour well-preserved. Collar seven bands of light blue, light green and white outlined in black, with a few traces remaining of bright blue. Folded cloths in hands white. Plain kilt with knotted belt white with red detail and outline.

STATUE 7

Pls. 24, 29

Niche H = 1.34m.; W = .41-.43m.; D = sill .17m., ceiling .09m.(S) and .10m.(N)
Statue H = 1.36m.

Restoration has been carried out on the right shoulder and upper chest, a good portion of the kilt and the left hand. The head is quite well-preserved, although some plaster is missing, and the right foot clearly shows splayed toes.

Colour

Hair, brows black. Eye, pupil and outline black; white eyeballs shaded on either side of pupil with four fine horizontal lines of orange-red. Five bands preserved of the collar: top band white and light blue rectangles, narrow band of white, three broader bands light blue, light green and light blue, vertical spacers now white. Folded cloth in right hand white. Kilt yellow and white with details, virtually identical to Nos. 2 and 4, preserved of belt, buckle, belt tab, ties and hanging beads.[286]

STATUE 8

Pls. 24, 29

Niche H = 1.36m.(S) and 1.37m.(N); W = .44m.; D = sill .17m., ceiling .10m.
Statue H = 1.37m.

The right side of the face is damaged and repair has been carried out on the right shoulder, upper chest and the legs between the knees and the ankles. Much of the plaster has gone from the kilt. The clenched right hand is roughly modelled with no indication in relief or paint of the cloth held in both hands of all other statues.

Colour

Hair and eye details black. A few broken lines of collar on left shoulder include traces of bright cobalt blue. Kilt patches of white; some belt and buckle details in black and red outline; belt tab yellow with horizontal red lines; ties red, two bands at ends with traces of light green.

---

286 Much more of the kilt, with all of the beads hanging from the belt, was preserved at the time de Rachewiltz published his report (ibid, pls. 10:2; 11:2).

STATUE 9

Pls. 24, 30

Niche H = 1.36m.; W = .43m.; D = sill .15m., ceiling .09m.
Statue H = 1.37m.

Neither of the two statues on the north wall, close to the entrance, is as well-preserved as those on the east. The surface of statue 9 is weathered and flaky with very little remaining of the painted plaster and recent repair to upper left chest. The head and face have suffered considerably and retain virtually no detail or colour. A red vertical guideline down the centre of the chest and kilt and a horizontal red line across the chest are visible where the plaster has fallen away.

Colour

Fragments of black on hair and of red on face, upper body and legs. Collar traces of blue and white at shoulder, possibly like Nos. 3 and 7. Kilt red outline only.

STATUE 10

Pls. 24, 30

Niche H = 1.36m.(E) and 1.35m.(W); W = .42m.; D = sill .15m., ceiling .07m.(E) and .06m.(W)
Statue H = 1.35m.

The statue is in a poor state of preservation and the upper part of both arms have been restored. Remarkably, the feet are more completely preserved on this statue than most others and show the splayed toes and outlines of rounded toenails.

Colour

Wig, eye outline and brows black. Kilt white. Folded cloth in hand white.

West Wall

Pls. 31-35, 36b, 37, 41

Cut into the west wall, north of the recess adjacent to the false door, are four niches, each containing a single rock-cut statue, but there is clear evidence that the original plan intended a total of seven statues in this wall. Reasonably well cut, the completed niches average .62m. in width and 1.62m. in height with a sill .45m. above the floor and are separated by piers .42m. (av.) wide. The piers were designed to include a frame with cavetto cornice, which is fully carved only around the first niche on the south and the south side of the adjacent niche. Red guidelines defining the torus, cornice and sides of the frames are partially preserved around this and the other two niches. There is no evidence of any inscriptions.

Each of the four niches of the west wall holds a life-size engaged statue, all standing with their feet together. The figures, three males and one female, have similar proportions to those on the east wall but differ in some detail as well as size.[287] Although not identified, it is probable that the male statues represent *Jrw-kꜣ-Ptḥ* and that of the female his wife. The two southernmost niches, but not the northern two, were cut to their full depth between the arms and torsos of the figures. A sandy pinkish plaster was used to repair flaws in the rock on statues 1, 2 and 4, as well as other areas of the east wall. There is evidence that statues 1 and 2, the most complete, were plastered with a pinky-cream overcoat in preparation for painting but, as only small fragments of this plaster remain, it is unknown if colour was applied.

STATUE 1

Pls. 31-32

Niche H = 1.62m.; W = .62m.; D = sill .24m., ceiling .13m.
Statue H = 1.60m. Shoulder W = .515m.

The southernmost standing male figure, almost certainly representing *Jrw-kꜣ-Ptḥ*, is the most completely finished of the four statues on this wall. Poor quality rock necessitated repair in plaster to the upper part of the head above the brows prior to carving. The figure stands with feet together and arms hanging straight beside the body, the hands clenched around a folded cloth. He wears a flared shoulder-length wig, parted in the middle and exposing the ear lobes, and a plain kilt with a buckle and belt tab. The face, with some damage to the nose and chin, is squarish in shape with broad cheeks and full lips. The broad-shouldered torso is well-modelled with the clavicle, breasts, vertical abdominal muscle and navel distinguished. Bicep and lower arm musculature is shown, and the knees and shin bones are indicated on the legs. The toes and bottom of the right fist are damaged. There are faint traces of red, perhaps the original guidelines, on the left nipple and the navel area, and some of the original plaster coating can be seen on the left shoulder, both arms and hands, chest and kilt.

STATUE 2

Pls. 31, 33, 36b

Niche H = 1.63m.; W = .62m.; D = sill .25m.(S) and .22m.(N), ceiling .16m.(S) and .14m.(N)
Statue H = 1.58m. Shoulder W = .48m.

The female figure in this niche, presumably the tomb owner's wife, stands with feet together, the left arm hanging beside the body and the right arm bent at the elbow to lie across the upper body with the palm flat on the left breast. Like statue 1, the upper part of the head was repaired at the time of sculpting and the eyes, forehead and upper part of the wig were carved in plaster. The woman wears a flared shoulder length wig parted in the middle which covers the ears and a long

287 The muscular body with different detail from those on east wall suggested to de Rachewiltz that they may have been executed by a different artist (ibid, 27).

dress (no indication of straps) which stops somewhat above the ankles. The cheeks are rounded and full, the eyes deeply set, the lips straight and full, with naso-labial creases and the philtrum above upper lip indicated. The clavicle is not modelled, but the breasts are distinguished as is the Y-line of the groin. The right hand lying across the breast is fully modelled, including rounded nails but details of the left arm, hanging open at side, are less clear. Both arms are roughly shaped, and shin bone lines as well as the separation of the legs are visible through the dress. The feet are weathered and shapeless and the toes damaged. Modern restoration can be seen on the right elbow, forearms, small finger and a portion of the (lower right) dress as well as the north side of the niche. This statue is not as finely smoothed as No. 1, with some small chisel marks ca .01cm. wide still visible, but traces remain of a plaster coating on the dress and both arms.

STATUE 3

Pls. 31, 34

Niche H = 1.63m.; W = .64m. at sill and .63m. at ceiling; D = sill .23m., ceiling .12m.
Statue H = 1.60m. Shoulder W = .55m.

The third statue, of a standing male figure with feet together, arms beside the body and clenched fists holding a cloth, is largely unfinished. Chisel marks are visible on most surfaces, those on the torso and arms ca .025-.030m. wide. The identity is uncertain, but the figure may represent *Jrw-kꜣ-Ptḥ*. The figure is basically only roughed out, with little attempt at modelling except the hair and upper facial details. Presumably due to its unfinished state, the measurement from top of the wig to chin of .24m. is considerably more than the .20-.21m. of the other statues on this wall. Unlike the other two male figures on the west wall, this statue wears a rounded cap wig, about .06m. above the shoulders, with no ears showing. The face is broad and flattish, with some shaping of the eyes, upper cheeks and nose but only vague indications of mouth and chin details. Below the neck the clavicle is suggested by a rough horizontal line. With little shape the arms exhibit no musculature and the fists no detail. The kilt is not indicated, the two legs are barely defined and the feet, still just a stone block, are not distinguished. Outlines in red paint remain on the head, wig, neck, torso and legs, as does part of the red guideline for the torso median line.

STATUE 4

Pls. 31, 35

Niche H = 1.61m.(S) and 1.63m.(N); W = .62m.; D = sill .27m.(S) and .25m.(N), ceiling .12m.
Statue H = 1.60m. Shoulder W = .53m.

Another standing male figure is very similar to statue 1 but not as well-finished, with little attempt at smoothing except on the face, shoulders and wig. The shoulder, chest and waist are broader than No. 1, all by .03m., and the face is slightly longer. Small traces of red paint, presumably guidelines, remain under the chin and on the torso. Fine chisel marks are visible on the well-modelled face; other chisel marks on the body from shoulder to kilt hem are .015m. wide and on the less-worked legs .020m. The statue wears a flared shoulder-length wig, cut at a sharper angle than No. 1, parted in the middle with the ear lobes exposed, and a plain kilt with no belt tab. The eyes have no detail, the nose is straight, broad and rounded, the naso-labial creases are defined as is the philtrum above the upper lip of a broad and full mouth. The clavicle, breasts and vertical abdominal muscle are modelled, but the arms are only roughly shaped, the right hand holding a cloth and the left broken. Chunky legs, not fully separated, have little shape and squarish feet, the toes of right foot broken. Original repair with coarse pinky plaster can be seen on the chest and left knee, and recent plaster restoration on the left hand and foot as well as at the top and sides of the niche.

West Wall, north

Pls. 37, 41

The surface of the west wall north of these statues was roughly smoothed and coated with a sandy, pinkish plaster, most of which has now disappeared. This wall area retains, however, some broken lines of red pigment which clearly indicate plans for an additional three niches. Horizontal guidelines for the torus moulding and cornice are partially preserved across the top of the wall from above the northernmost niche to .95m. south of the west entrance thickness, where the cornice line is clearly visible.[288] Some vertical lines remaining indicate the sides of niches and frames and, in two places, the lines of a figure. One shows the elbow of a right arm and the waist, the other a small part of probably the upper left arm. These broken lines, and their placement, clearly indicate that the original intent was to cut into this wall three more niches with the same measurements as the four existing ones, and to sculpt three additional engaged figures.

Commentary

Nine of the statues are fully sculpted, smoothed, plastered and painted while the remainder are unfinished, left in various stages of completion including some in painted outline. All are of particular interest in illustrating different steps involved in producing engaged statuary. The first was the accurate measuring and drawing any necessary guidelines for the niche(s) and an outline of the figure(s) in frontal form in red paint. Such painted outlines are partially preserved on the southern part of the east wall, where overlapping lines indicate several corrections to the figures and the niches, and on the northern part of the west wall where the lines appear to have been measured and placed with greater accuracy. The initial cutting blocked out very roughly the contours of the figure and the depth of the niche. This procedure is illustrated by the incomplete statue No. 1 on the east wall which also shows that the main features of this figure were redrawn in a broad line of black paint to assist the sculptor in the next stage.

The statues on the west wall demonstrate the successive stages of chiselling with tools of varying widths, getting narrower to progressively refine the shape and

---

288 An illustration of some of this plaster described by de Rachewiltz as "found on the ceiling" is surely a result of the photograph being published upside down (*Irw-k3-Ptḥ*, 28, pl. 26).

gradually define musculature, facial and other details.[289] Statue No. 3 is further advanced than No. 1 on the east wall, the figure being more clearly defined but with little shaping, no separation of legs and feet and virtually no indication of any detail except on the upper part of the head. No. 4 has finer chisel marks, and is well-shaped with modelling and details, but little smoothing. The sculpting of Nos. 1 and 2 appears complete, well-modelled, smoothed and with evidence of a plaster coating but no painted decoration. Major flaws in the rock were repaired with a hard plaster prior to the final carving, seen clearly on the heads of Nos. 1 and 2, the right arm of the latter and the chest of No. 4. Red guidelines on the unfinished statue No. 3 on the west wall and on No. 9 on the north wall where the painted plaster has fallen surely represent additional lines to guide the artist producing the final decoration. The sculpted and smoothed high-relief figures were coated with a finer gypsum plaster to cover imperfections and provide an even surface. Final modelling and painted details were executed on this plaster base, similar to the procedure followed in the carving and decoration of wall reliefs, as demonstrated in the well-preserved finished figures Nos. 2-10 on the north and east walls.

Had the original design of an additional five statues been fully executed in *Jrw-kꜣ-Ptḥ*'s tomb, it would have resulted in 19 rock-cut statues, a very large number in absolute terms and perhaps surprising for a man of his status. Not a common feature in the Old Kingdom, the use of engaged statuary was initiated in rock-cut tombs of important individuals at Giza in mid-Dynasty 4, and is attested at that site and in Upper Egypt in Dynasty 5 and the first half of Dynasty 6, but seldom at Saqqara. Engaged statues are generally contained in rock-cut niches which may hold single, double or multiple images.[290] The first tomb known to include rock-cut statuary in its decorative program is that of Queen *Mr.s-ꜥnḫ* III at Giza in the latter part of Dynasty 4 which has 20 figures in six different niches, 14 standing female family members and six seated scribes.[291] Engaged statues numbering ten or more are documented in another five tombs at Giza[292] and seven in Upper Egypt,[293] all but three[294] with probable dates prior to Dynasty 6. The only Old Kingdom tombs with a larger number than the 19 planned for *Jrw-kꜣ-Ptḥ* 's tomb are those of *Mr.s-ꜥnḫ* III, *Kꜣ.j-ḫr-Ptḥ* in Dynasty 6 and also at Giza with a grand total of 29,[295] and *Mmj* at El-Hawawish in Upper Egypt, dated to the reign of Djedkare, with 24.[296] In none of these tombs were all the statues cut in individual

---

289 For comments on materials and methods of sculptors and pictures of some of their tools see Ziegler in *Egyptian Art*, 280, Nos. 73-75.

290 Kendall, *Studies Dunham*, 104-105 n.1.

291 Dunham - Simpson, *Mersyankh III*, pls. 6, 8, 9a-b, 11b-c.

292 *Ḏdj*, 11 (Hassan, *Gîza* 1, 86-87, pls. 53-54); Mastaba F, 12+ (ibid, vol. 3, 72-74); *Dbḥn*, 17 (ibid, vol. 4, 167, 172-73, figs. 113, 120; Lepsius, *Denkmäler* II, pl. 27); *ꜥnḫ-m-ꜥ-Rꜥ*, 15 (Kendall, *Studies Dunham*, 105 n.1; Smith, *HESPOK*, pl. 57d); *Kꜣ.j-ḫr-Ptḥ*, 29 (Kendall, *Studies Dunham*, 104-114).

293 *Nj-kꜣ-ꜥnḫ*, 16 (Frazer, *ASAE* 3 [1902], 122-25, 128, pls. 1, 3); *Kp*, 13+ (ibid, 71-72); *Srf-kꜣ.j*, 11 (Davies, *Sheikh Saïd*, 12, pl. 3); *Mrw/Bbj*, 10 (ibid, pls. 18, 21); *Ttj-ꜥnḫ/Jm-ḥtp*, 11 (ibid, 33-34, pl. 27); *Kꜣ.j-ḫnt*, 13 (El-Khouli - Kanawati, *El-Hammamiya*, 37-38, 40, 44-47, pls. 7, 9a, 16c); *Mmj*, 24 (Kanawati, *El-Hawawish* 5, 40-41, pls. 7a, 8a, fig. 11).

294 Kendall, *Studies Dunham*, 104-114; Davies, *Sheikh Saïd*, 33-34, pls. 18, 21, 27.

295 Kendall, *Studies Dunham*, 104-114.

296 Kanawati, *El-Hawawish* 5, 40-41, pls. 7a, 8a, fig. 11.

niches,[297] a feature encountered infrequently and generally in tombs with a smaller number of statues early in Dynasty 6.[298] Rare examples of a large number of single engaged figures in individual niches are, however, attested at Saqqara.

On the basis of present evidence, rock-cut statuary is found at Saqqara in only two other tombs,[299] both with proposed dates in the latter part of Dynasty 5 and thus closely contemporary with that *Jrw-kꜣ-Ptḥ*. The tomb of *Qd-ns*, with two open courts, an offering room and serdab cut in rock, has in the second court "about ten niches", probably on the north and east walls, holding statues of the tomb owner and his son.[300] As no details are reported and presumably no inscriptions survived, it is unknown whether each niche held an individual statue, but likely with the dimensions given for the walls. Found by Mariette at the turn of the twentieth century, the exact location of this tomb, reportedly somewhere east of the Step Pyramid,[301] is no longer known. Beside the entrance to the South Ibis Galleries at North Saqqara a damaged chamber discovered by Emery in 1964-65 has a row of nine niches separated by piers holding individual rock-cut statues, six male and three female.[302] Reported as unfinished, the photographs indicate quite well-modelled, but weathered, figures and, although smaller, not unlike those of *Jrw-kꜣ-Ptḥ*.[303] Any colour, if ever applied, no longer exists and no inscriptions were found.

Although statues depicted in wall scenes are frequently shown standing in a shrine with cavetto cornice,[304] it is seldom that a statue niche in a tomb is surrounded by a frame and cornice. With the exception of *Jrw-kꜣ-Ptḥ*, documented examples in rock tombs are all at Giza. The feature first appears late in Dynasty 4 in one of the earliest tombs to use engaged statuary, that of *Dbḥn*, around a single niche holding 13 striding statues.[305] It is found in the latter part of Dynasty 5 in

---

297 The tomb of *Ttj-ꜥnḫ/Jm-ḥtp* at Sheikh Said is in a poor state of preservation and was extensively altered as a result of habitation by early Coptic hermits. As many of the eleven niches have suffered damage and little remains of the engaged figures, it is not possible to ascertain from the report how many of the niches may have held a single statue (see Davies, *Sheikh Saïd*, 31-34, pl. 27).

298 See at Memphis *Jdw*, 6 (Simpson, *Qar and Idu*, pls. 21-22, 23a-b); in Upper Egypt *H̱nw-kꜣ.j*, 7 (Frazer, *ASAE* 3 [1902], 74, pl. 2); Tomb No. 6, 5 (Davies, *Sheikh Saïd*, 35, pl. 32).

299 No details are available of a tomb with engaged statues reportedly encountered in the recent Saqqara excavations of Dr. A. Zivie.

300 Mariette, *Mastabas*, 403 (E10); dated by Mariette to Dynasty 6 and more recently to end Dynasty 5-beginning Dynasty 6 (Baer, *Rank and Title*, 137; Harpur, *Decoration*, 276).

301 Smith in Reisner, *Tomb Development*, 410.

302 *JEA* 51 [1965], 6, pl. 2:2; idem, *JEA* 52 [1966], 5, pl. 1:4; Martin, *Hetepka*, 9-10, 115, 117, pl. 40a-c. The reports give broad dating of Old Kingdom, early Old Kingdom and late Old Kingdom.

303 Good copies of the photographs published by Martin were generously supplied by Prof. Harry Smith who provided additional information together with his personal assessment that the tomb "might well be of 4th Dyn date, and almost certainly was not later than 5th Dynasty" (private correspondence 17/6 and 29/7/97).

304 For example Lepsius, *Denkmäler* II, pl. 78b; Épron - Wild, *Ti* 1, pl. 52; Duell, *Mereruka*, pls. 39, 97A; Dunham - Simpson, *Mersyankh III*, fig. 5; Moussa - Altenmüller, *Nianchchnum*, pls. 16-17; Verner, *Ptahshepses*, photo 111; Ziegler, *Akhethetep*, 106, 108.

305 Lepsius, *Denkmäler* II, pl. 27; Hassan, *Gîza* 4, 167.

the tomb of *Ḫww-wr*, enclosing two niches, each holding a single statue, and an intervening doorway.[306] A frame with cavetto cornice surrounds each of the four statue niches holding a total of eight standing figures in the tomb of *Nj-wḏꜣ-Ptḥ*,[307] who may be close in time to *Ḫww-wr* and *Jrw-kꜣ-Ptḥ* in the second half of Dynasty 5. The tomb of *Kꜣ.j-ḫr-Ptḥ*, dated in the first half of Dynasty 6, makes use of a cavetto cornice on five niches, each with multiple images.[308] It may be noted that the large statue of *Mrrw-kꜣ.j* in his mastaba constructed at Saqqara stands in a niche with an inscribed frame and torus moulding which, although the upper part is gone, very probably was surmounted by a cavetto cornice.[309]

In general engaged statues are poorly preserved. The conglomerate limestone in which they were carved lacks the finer, compact quality of the quarried blocks from which statues in the round were produced. Few Old Kingdom rock-cut statues either at the capital or in the provinces have escaped extensive weathering or damage and, with the loss of the plaster coating, both sculpted and painted detail have largely disappeared. The abundance of colour and detail preserved on the statues of *Jrw-kꜣ-Ptḥ* is, therefore, unique and of great value in assessing the artistry and style of rock-cut figures. The only other engaged statuary of the Old Kingdom which retains some, although a small portion, of its painted decoration is in the tomb of *Jdw* at Giza in the first half of Dynasty 6.[310] Five of the six male figures in the east wall, the other a child, exhibit some stylistic similarities to the statues on the north and east walls of *Jrw-kꜣ-Ptḥ*. They have the same rigid stance with the feet together and the arms beside the bodies, a folded cloth in each hand, short rounded wigs[311] and the same type of kilts with painted details of the belt and hanging beads. Also like *Jrw-kꜣ-Ptḥ*, all are placed in individual niches separated by piers with inscriptions and a horizontal line of text above. Similar inscriptions are partially preserved around several damaged statue niches in tombs at Sheikh Said dated early in Dynasty 6.[312]

Some comparisons can, however, be made with figures sculpted in the round which preserve facial and body modelling and painted details. For example, while it is unknown if moustaches were painted on other engaged figures, this feature, attested also in Dynasties 3 and 4, is found in royal and private statuary of Dynasty 5. A moustache is depicted on statues of Userkaf[313] and Neferefre[314] discovered

---

306 Hassan, *Gîza* 5, 249, fig. 107, pl. 27.

307 Abu-Bakr, *Giza*, figs. 20, 95A, C-E, pls. 61-64. A possible date of mid-late Dynasty 5 is suggested by chairs on which the tomb owner and his wife are seated having no cushion (Cherpion, *Mastabas et hypogées*, 26: Criterion 1) and two false doors lacking a cavetto cornice, the type most commonly attested from the beginning of Dynasty 6 (ibid, 75, 197-98: Criterion 54).

308 Kendall, *Studies Dunham*, 109, figs. 5-7, 9-10, 12.

309 Duell, *Mereruka*, pl. 147.

310 Simpson, *Qar and Idu*, pls. 21-22, 23a-b. Male flesh patches of red; hair and eye detail black; bracelets blue, collars and belt traces of red, blue and green.

311 Not "shoulder length" as reported (ibid, 24).

312 Davies, *Sheikh Saïd*, pl. 21.

313 Saleh - Sourouzian, *Museum Cairo*, Cat. No. 35 = JdE 90220.

314 Verner, *BIFAO* 85 [1985], 271-72, 274, 280, pls. 44-46, 47A, 58; Saleh - Sourouzian, *Museum Cairo*, Cat. No. 38 = JdE 98171.

at Abusir and on another which may represent Unis or Teti.[315] Perhaps becoming fashionable following its royal use in the first half of Dynasty 5, a moustache is seen in the second half of Dynasty 5 on private statues with a provenance of Giza[316] and more frequently Saqqara, including those of *Wr-jr-n.j*,[317] *Ptḥ-špss*,[318] *Sḫm-kꜣ.j*,[319] *Nj-mꜣꜥt-sd*,[320] *Kꜣ.j-m-ḥzt*,[321] *ꜣḫt-ḥtp*.[322] Of unknown provenance, but probably Giza or Saqqara, is another Fifth Dynasty statue with a moustache of *ꜥnḫ-ḥꜣ.f* who bears, like *Jrw-kꜣ-Ptḥ*, the title *qbḥ-nmt pr-ꜥꜣ*.[323]

Preserved on a number of statues in the round is a kilt painted half yellow and half white with an elaborate belt,[324] but seldom with an additional adornment of hanging strands of beads with tassels.[325] Attested in a royal context as early as Narmer,[326] beaded decoration occurs on kilts of Fourth and Fifth Dynasty kings,[327] and appears to have been adapted for private use in the latter part of Dynasty 5. Such details are preserved on a statue from Giza of *Mnw-nfr*,[328] and on those from Saqqara of *Kꜣ.j-m-qd*,[329] *Kꜣ.j-ḫ(w)j.f*[330] and *Mṯṯj*.[331] The statues of *Jrw-kꜣ-Ptḥ*, *Kꜣ.j-ḫ(w)j.f* and *Kꜣ.j-m-qd*, the last recovered from the tomb of *Wr-jr-n.j* whom he served as *ḥm-kꜣ*, show four strands of beads; most others have five or six, but one figure of *Mṯṯj* has seven.[332] In Dynasty 6 a beaded kilt is found on the engaged statues of *Jdw* at Giza mentioned above, and on a free-standing statue of *Jpj/ꜥnḫ-jr.s* from Saqqara.[333] Also in Dynasty 6, a wooden statue of *Nj-ꜥnḫ-Ppjj-km* from Meir shows a kilt with a slightly different style of ornamentation,[334] the belt and beaded attachment clearly illustrated in a scene of jewellery production

315 Romano, *Critères de datation*, 275-76, figs. 70-71 = Freer Gallery, Washington DC, 38.11.

316 E.g., *Msj* from G2009 (Smith, *HESPOK*, 69, pl. 24b = Cairo JdE 38670); *ꜣḫw* (Abu-Bakr, *Giza*, pls. 50b, 51); *Jttj* from G7391 (Curto, *Gli Scavi*, pls. 9-10); *Mr-sw-ꜥnḫ* (Saleh - Sourouzian, *Museum Cairo*, Cat. No. 51 = JdE 66617); *Nfr-ḥr-n-Ptḥ* (ibid, Cat. No. 56 = JdE 87804). For a rare example in Dynasty 6 see Ziegler, *Statues*, No. 30, 108-111.

317 Borchardt, *Statuen* 1, 172, pl. 58 = CG 272 (D20).

318 Ibid, 47-48, 139-40, 143, pls. 14, 43, 45 = CG 54, 207, 214 (C10).

319 Ziegler, *Statues*, No. 36, 131-34.

320 Borchardt, *Statuen* 1, 51-52, 69-70, 99-100, pls. 15, 20, 30 = CG 58, 88, 133 (D56); Saleh - Sourouzian, *Museum Cairo*, Cat. No. 48 = CG 133.

321 Ibid, Cat. No. 54 = JdE 44174.

322 Cairo Museum JdE 93164, JdE 93170.

323 Borchardt, *Statuen* 1, 141, pl. 44 = CG 210.

324 Many examples show the yellow part as pleated, a type of kilt which is attested, according to Staehlin, chiefly in the Fifth Dynasty (*Tracht*, 13).

325 For a brief discussion of strings of beads worn with kilts see ibid, 30-31.

326 Hanging beads adorn the royal kilt on both sides of the Narmer Palette (Saleh - Sourouzian, *Museum Cairo*, Cat. No. 8).

327 Hassan, *Gîza* 10, pl. 7A (Khufu); Borchardt, *Sá3ḥu-Reꜥ* 2, 51, pl. 39; idem, *Ne-User-Reꜥ*, 38-39, fig. 18.

328 Tomb G 2421 of *Mnw-nfr* is largely unpublished and I am grateful to Dr. E. Brovarski for photocopies of expedition photographs of the statues now in Boston Museum of Fine Arts.

329 Saleh - Sourouzian, *Museum Cairo*, Cat. No. 47 = CG 119.

330 Borchardt, *Statuen* 1, 170-71, pl. 57 = CG 268.

331 Kaplony, *Methethi*, 56, 60-62, 64-68 (Nos. 11, 13: Brooklyn 50.77 and 53.222) = Russmann, *MDAIK* 51 [1995], pl. 55.

332 See ibid, pl. 55b.

333 Borchardt, *Statuen* 1, 43, pl. 12 = CG 47.

334 Ibid, 52-53, pl. 15 = CG 60.

in the tomb of *Nj-ꜥnḫ-Ppjj-km*'s son, *Ppjj-ꜥnḫ/Ḥnj-km*.[335] This same type of kilt decoration appears in wall scenes at Saqqara in the tombs of viziers who served Teti, worn by *ꜥnḫ-m-ꜥ-Ḥr* and *Ḫntj-kꜣj/Jḫḫj*,[336] and is illustrated in the tomb at South Saqqara of *Ḫw-bꜣw* who is dated to late Pepy I-early Pepy II.[337] Very recently, fieldwork in the Teti Cemetery by the Australian Centre for Egyptology recovered from the burial chamber of another of Teti's senior officials, *Nj-kꜣw-Jzzj*, three bell-shaped gold objects which appear to be tassels together with three lozenge-shaped carnelian beads.[338] These finds presumably formed part of a similar kilt adornment.

There are other similarities between the rock-cut statues of *Jrw-kꜣ-Ptḥ* and the wooden ones of *Mṯṯj*, the latter dated to the transition period between Dynasties 5 and 6 and considered by Russmann to show early manifestations of what she calls a "second style" of Old Kingdom sculpture with its origins at Saqqara.[339] The figures of *Mṯṯj* wearing elaborate kilts with hanging strands of beads are stylistically differentiated by Russmann: one type, whose short rounded wig and facial features may be compared to those of *Jrw-kꜣ-Ptḥ*, has traditional Fifth Dynasty characteristics of a round face, broad shoulders and sturdy legs; the other has a proportionately larger head, more elongated face, narrower shoulders and smaller waist which are indicative of the second, Sixth Dynasty style.[340] While the Fifth Dynasty style predominates in *Jrw-kꜣ-Ptḥ*'s statuary some hints of the "second style" may be seen, particularly in the oversized head and narrow waist of Nos. 2 and 10.

In addition to the kilt adornment of belt and hanging beads, the design, details and colouring of the broad collars on the statues of *Jrw-kꜣ-Ptḥ* and *Mṯṯj* are very alike. The collar with nine bands on *Jrw-kꜣ-Ptḥ*'s No. 4 is similar to that of Brooklyn 50.77, and the collars with spacers on Nos. 2 and 7 resemble that on Brooklyn 53.222.[341] The black markings on the chest of No. 2 remain somewhat of an enigma, as no exact parallels can be found.[342] Two statues of *Mṯṯj*, one wearing a kilt with hanging beads like *Jrw-kꜣ-Ptḥ*, show banded straps emerging below the broad collar which, presumably hanging over the shoulders, fall in a moderate v-shape towards the navel.[343] Similar straps but no collar are depicted on an anonymous male figure in the Louvre clad in a long stiffened kilt and dated to

---

335 Blackman, *Meir* 5, pl. 16.

336 Respectively, Kanawati - Hassan, *Teti Cemetery* 2, pls. 10, 44; James, *Khentika*, pl. 16.

337 Maspero, *Trois années de fouilles*, pl. 1.

338 Kanawati - Abder-Raziq, *Teti Cemetery* 6, 67, pl. 2d.

339 *MDAIK* 51 [1995], 269-79, esp. 274-76, pl. 55. For *Mṯṯj*'s dating see ibid, 274; Baer, *Rank and Title*, 83; Cherpion, *Mastabas et hypogées*, 94. Others have proposed late Dynasty 5 (Kaplony, *Methethi*, 7), Dynasty 6 (Ziegler, *Catalogue des stèles*, 120-23), Pepy I (Harpur, *Decoration*, 274) and the end of the Old Kingdom (Munro, *GM* 59 [1982], 98; Altenmüller, *MDAIK* 36 [1986], 346).

340 *MDAIK* 51 [1995], 274.

341 For detailed descriptions see Kaplony, *Methethi*, 61-62, 66-67.

342 Called a tattoo by de Rachewiltz (*Irw-k3-Ptḥ*, 10). No adornment with the same form is included in the discussion on jewellery by Staehlin (*Tracht*, 100-139).

343 Kaplony, *Methethi*, 66-80 (No. 13 = Brooklyn 53.222, No. 14 = Kansas City, 51-1).

Dynasty 6.[344] These straps also appear in wall scenes in Dynasty 6 at Saqqara,[345] and in Upper Egypt at Meir.[346] Of these examples only one statue of *Mṯtj* and the sons and attendants of the tomb owners at Meir are depicted in short kilts, as worn by *Jrw-kꜣ-Ptḥ*, the others wearing long stiffened kilts.

VI DECORATION AND COLOUR CONVENTIONS

In preparation for decoration, the rock surfaces of the walls were roughly hammered and smoothed, using a coarse pinky plaster for repairs where necessary (fractures, breaks), followed by a thin application of creamy gypsum plaster. On this surface the decoration was drafted in red paint and the scenes executed in shallow low relief and coated with a fine white plaster prior to painting. Horizontal texts across the east and north walls, vertical texts on the piers between the statue niches as well as the decoration on the limestone false door are in incised relief.

Some elements of the wall decoration, including all four registers of marsh activities and a good many details, are rendered in paint only and, as well as unfinished sections, there is evidence of some corrections or alterations in the layout. These have either already been noted in comments on individual scenes or will be mentioned below.

The scenes of marsh activities on the east wall, while composed and organised in a manner typical of late Dynasty 5-early Dynasty 6, show a number of anomalies which may be related to a change in the design of the decorative program. The lower two registers align on the south with two registers of boats, but the upper two have neither any linear connection with, nor any clear separation from, the adjacent decoration. The stern of the large papyrus boat in the fowling scene is tucked under the register line of the butchery scene as is also the small skiff. The bow of the skiff and part of the harpoon are missing due to the niche holding an unfinished engaged statue. It is doubtful if there could have been room for more than a token papyrus thicket in front of the fowling boat. Beneath the fowling scene the representation of cattle fording, facing north like the small papyrus skiff above, should have either included a boat or herdsman (with the calf) leading the cattle (with the two boats behind) or the cattle and men in the boats should face the opposite direction.

The horizontal inscription reading from the south end concludes with *jmꜣḫ(w)*, lacking the name of the tomb owner, and resumes to the north of the panel with marsh scenes directly above the incomplete statue. One wonders, however, if this figure was part of the original design since the adjacent statues on the east wall and those on the north are complete, fully sculpted, plastered and painted in detail.

---

344 Ziegler, *Statues*, Cat. No. 55, 195-97.

345 Worn by a brother of *ꜥnḫ-m-ꜥ-Ḥr* (Kanawati - Hassan, *Teti Cemetery* 2, pl. 45).

346 Worn by *Nj-ꜥnḫ-Ppjj-km* and his son *Ppjj-ꜥnḫ/Ḥnj-km* and in the tomb of the latter by his son *Ḥnjjt* (Blackman, *Meir* 5, pls. 14, 26; in the latter scene the straps, but no collars, are worn by six bearers of furnishings approaching the tomb owner).

Above the finished statue adjacent to the roughly blocked-out figure is etched a cavetto cornice. Was the original plan to have seven statues on the east wall as on the west? The third group of butchers is directly above the cavetto cornice and first complete statue. Was the fourth butchery group which impinges on the fowling scene an unplanned addition, or do the unfinished marsh scenes in the centre of the wall represent some unexpected adjustment of the original decorative program to fit this space? Could the original intent have been to continue the horizontal inscription across the entire wall? One also wonders if any decoration was planned for the wall area between the two statues outlined in red and the serdab.

The background was painted a clear mid-blue-grey, best preserved at the north end of east wall, the lower left section of fowling scene, the two bottom registers of marsh activities and the southern section of the horizontal text. Remains of the same background paint can also be seen on the sills, ceilings and walls of the statue niches on the east wall as well as the piers separating them. The painted plaster at the south end of the east wall has fallen, leaving only faint incised lines of the original scene. There is no evidence of a frieze or of a dado on the walls, as scenes and statue niches are not far above the floor level. However a dado is painted on the false door, at the bottom of the jambs beneath the standing figures of the owner. The upper band, .03m high and retaining some red pigment, is separated by a narrow black horizontal line from the lower band, .04m. high and with no colour. Beneath, a band .08m. high to the base of the jamb shows remnants of black paint. Register lines and vertical columns on the false door are black.

Male figures in the wall scenes consistently have skin painted brown-red with hair, brow, eye details and outline in black. Kilts and loin-cloths are white and in most cases retain an orange-red outline. The collar of the seated tomb owner at the north end of the east wall shows traces of blue but no colour appears on his collars elsewhere, which retain only a white undercoat.

Paint only

NORTH WALL

chest behind last figure, top register

EAST WALL

Seated tomb owner and offerings:

inscription before face of tomb owner

tomb owner's mouth and chin (which do not follow relief carving)

stiffened pointed kilt of tomb owner and folded cloth in right hand, both a correction of the carved original which had a plain kilt and the right hand in a different position

central ewer and basin on chest in top register of piled offerings, an addition between the two original ewers whose carved outlines are larger than the painted areas, both being reduced in size in order to make space for the third vessel between them added in paint

Piled offerings:

marrows in all registers both north and south

grapes top register right, north end and in woven baskets lower register south end

onions adjacent to calf's head bottom register north end

Butchery: whetstones and cords
Marsh scenes: entire panel devoted to marsh activities in paint only
Boats: all rowlocks, ropes securing steering oars, matting of cabin, lashing detail on cabin supports and top and bottom yards, loops of braces at ends of top yards, cord held by pilot. Stays, ropes, oars, men carved in some painted in others. The first boat in each of registers 1-3 has more carved detail than the second

register 1, boat 1 (S) - part of awning, upper part of mast, some backstays, some oars, two figures seated forward of mast

register 1, boat 2 (N) - papyrus lashing on hull, mast, all stays (three still in red outline) and braces, rowlocks and securing lines; head, shoulders and staff of pilot, all seated crew, man with outstretched arms

register 2, boat 1 (S) - some stays and oars, tomb owner's staff, seated men facing aft

register 2, boat 2 (N) - mast, all stays and braces, seated men facing aft and some rowers, signalman, bowing figure, oars, staff of tomb owner

register 3, boat 1 (N) - seated figures, oars, signalman, bowing figure, bird(?) held over side of boat

register 3, boat 2 (S) - two oars

register 4 , both boats - details of cabins and cargo

WEST WALL:
inscriptions upper lintel false door

Black outline only
jar with stand and cover, offerings, east wall south
fowling scene, east wall
cattle in fording scene, east wall
partially cut statue No. 1, east wall

Red drafting lines
niche and statue outlines, west and east walls
cavetto cornice, partially carved above statue No. 2, east wall
horizontal guidelines on false door panel and dado, west wall

Pigments

Yellow	clear ochre
Brown	very dark ochre (shading on figs, oxtails, loaves)
Red	brown-red (flesh colour)
	orange-red
Green	light green
Blue	clear cobalt blue
	light aqua blue

Hieroglyphic signs

The signs of the horizontal text across the east and north walls are well-painted with good detail, but not the name and titles of the tomb owner elsewhere on the east wall. The signs in front of seated tomb owner at north end are in paint only, blue with black outline. The incised inscriptions on the piers between the statues on the east wall are, from south: 1) no text; 2) black; 3) black; 4) blue, black outline; 5) black; 6) black; 7) blue, black outline. The signs listed below are presented according to Gardiner's sign list, with one, in bold type, taken from *Hieroglyphica* I and two with no reference.

A20 Flesh orange-red; hair and eye black; kilt white with orange-red outline; staff yellow with orange-red outline

A40 Face yellow; hair, beard and eye black;, clothing white

D1 Face orange-red; hair and beard black; eye black on white ground

D2 Face yellow; hair eyes and neck black; mouth, nose, ear detail and outline red

D4 Black outline, eyeball shaded with orange-red horizontal stripes, pupil dark red with black outline and centre

D45 N) Arms orange-red; sceptre head white, handle yellow with dark red detail, outline dark red

S 1, 2) Arms red; sceptre head and handle yellow; details and outline red

F35 White with orange-red detail; two outlined in orange-red, one at south end dark red

F39 Orange-red with white

G7 Back, wing and tail blue with black tail feather detail and outline; head white with red neck and crest; neck ruff, head feathers and outline black; eye details, pupil and outline black; beak yellow with black outline; leg feathering white with red outline; legs and feet yellow with red outline, claw details black. Standard red; cloth white with black detail; feather light green with black details and outline

G17 Face white; ears, eyebrows, pupil black; eyes and nose red; head outlined in fine red dots (head feathering); breast white with black spots; body outline orange-red; wing yellow with red feather detail and outline; legs yellow outlined in red, claws black

G43 Body yellow; head and breast outline red; eye orange-red outlined in black; feather, wing details, tuft on tail and back outline black; beak and legs orange-red: N 1) black details on feet and orange-red centre to eye; N 2) red legs

G131B Body, head and legs same as G7. Standard blue outlined in black and red; feather white with red outline; base green with black detail and outline, hill red

I9 Yellow with white belly and red outline; ears, eyes and neck rings black

N26 N 1) Land red with black dots; base light green, outline black

N 2) Land pinky-red with cobalt blue and black dots; base green, outline black

S) Land red; base green, outline black

N31 Land dark red; edges light green with black outline

O21 N) Cornice, base and door red; frame lashing black on white; façade yellow with criss-cross lines red and orange-red and black dot where intersect

S) Cornice, base, frame, door orange-red; lashing black and white; façade yellow with criss-cross lines red and black

O49 S) Crossroads blue, outline black on white ground (triangles)

N 1) Same as S with red triangle inside white triangle

N 2) Same as S with black triangle inside white triangle

Q6 Yellow with red detail and outline

R4 Light green with black detail and outline; loaf yellow with red outline

R8 Flag and top of pole yellow with orange-red detail and outline (southernmost red outline); base of pole on one example green (others no colour preserved) with black diagonal lashing and outline

R11 From bottom 4 bands alternating light blue and green, then 3 bands of yellow, a band no colour, then yellow, blue, yellow, light green, yellow, blue, yellow; top blue; outlines all black

U1 Light green with black outline; teeth of one preserves white with black detail and outline

W17 Bottom of jars orange-red; top, neck and rim of jars black; caps white with red outline

W16 N) lower part of jar and stand red; spout and water black

N) Black, spots of red on black knife to indicate blood

Red

O29 (N) O34 S29

Orange-red

D21  D54  O29 (E)

Green - all light green with black outline, M17 and Q3 black detail

M17  M23  Q1  Q3  V4 

V30  Aa1 

Blue - all with black outline

N16 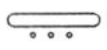 3 dots (carved-S) blue and (painted-N) black

N29  T20 X1 X8  (1 E) Z11 

Black

E15  O1 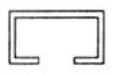 X1 X8  (2 E)

False door: No signs are outlined

Polychrome

A6  Flesh and jar orange-red; water blue

G43  Body yellow; legs orange-red

R8  Flag and upper part of pole yellow; lower part of pole green

W15  Jar, one orange-red, two red; tops and water blue

 Building blue; knife black

 Mouth orange-red, line blue

Orange-red

D21  D28  O29 F39 

Yellow

X1  (panel offering list)

Green

M12  M17  M23  Q3  U1 

V28  V31  Aa1 

Blue

O1 (panel) X1 (panel, left jamb)

Black inscriptions on upper lintel all black paint only

D4 N35 O1 W24 X1 (generally black but panel and left jamb blue, similar in short offering list yellow)

White

V6

INDEX

TITLES AND EPITHETS

PLATES

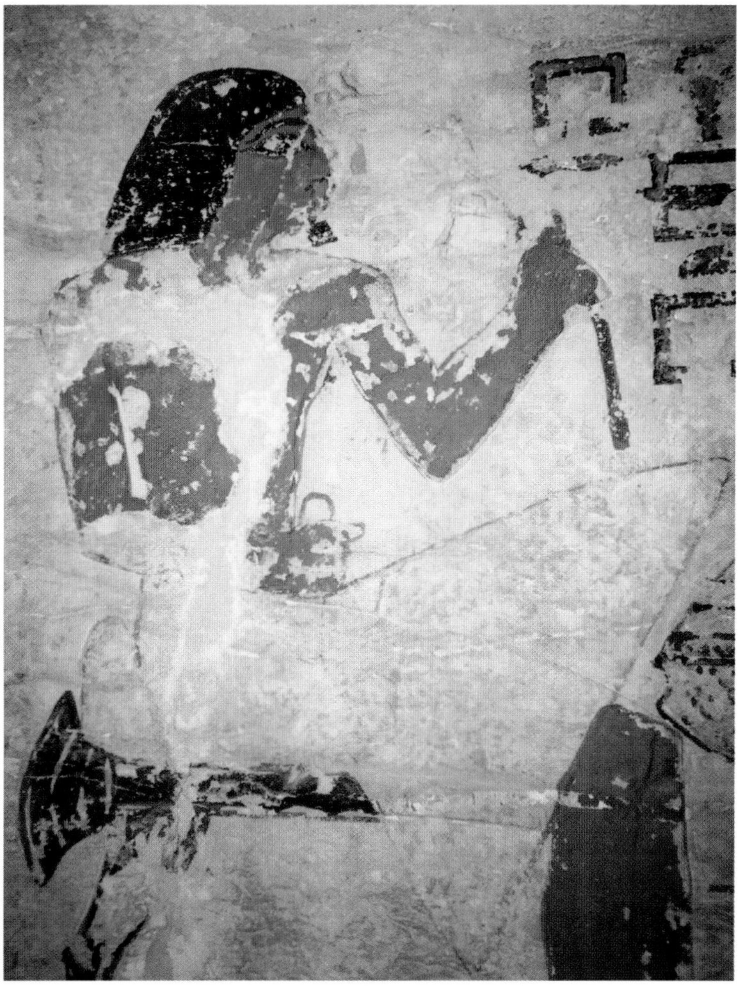

(a) North end, upper part, detail

(b) North, upper part, detail

Pl. 1. East Wall

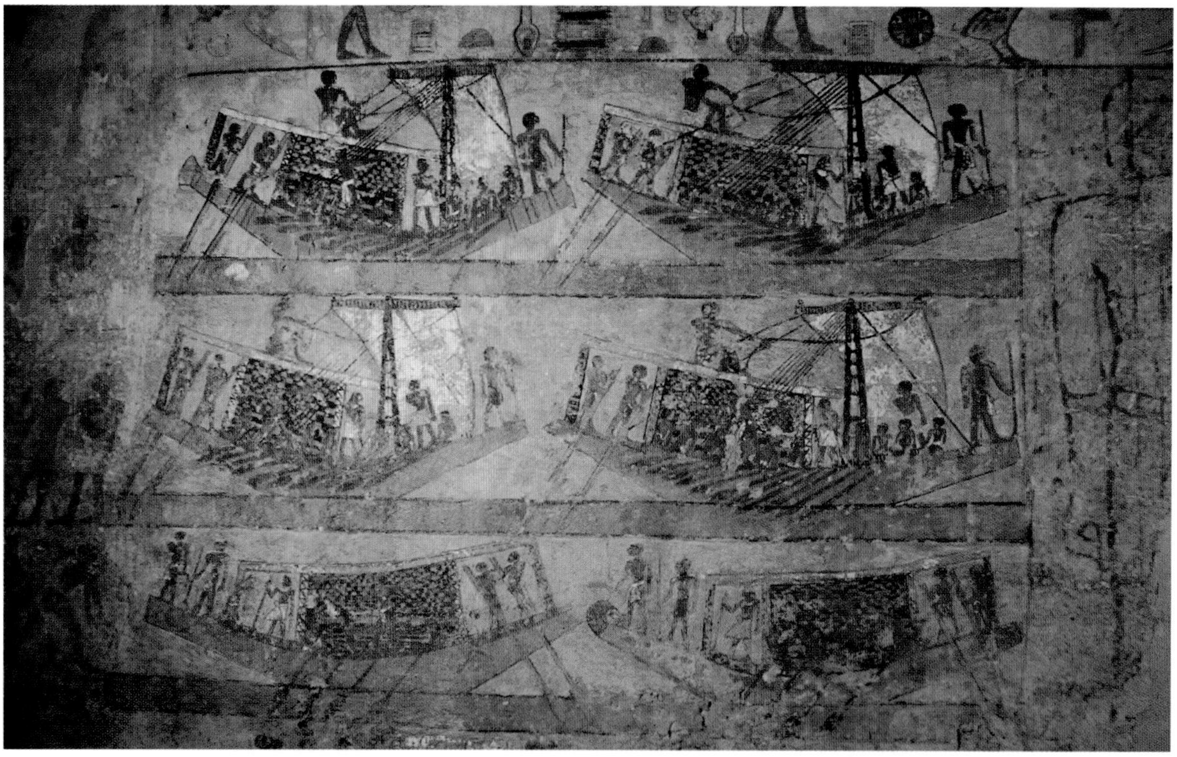

(a) Registers 1 to 3

(b) Register 1, detail

(c) Register 3, detail

Pl. 2. East wall, south, lower part

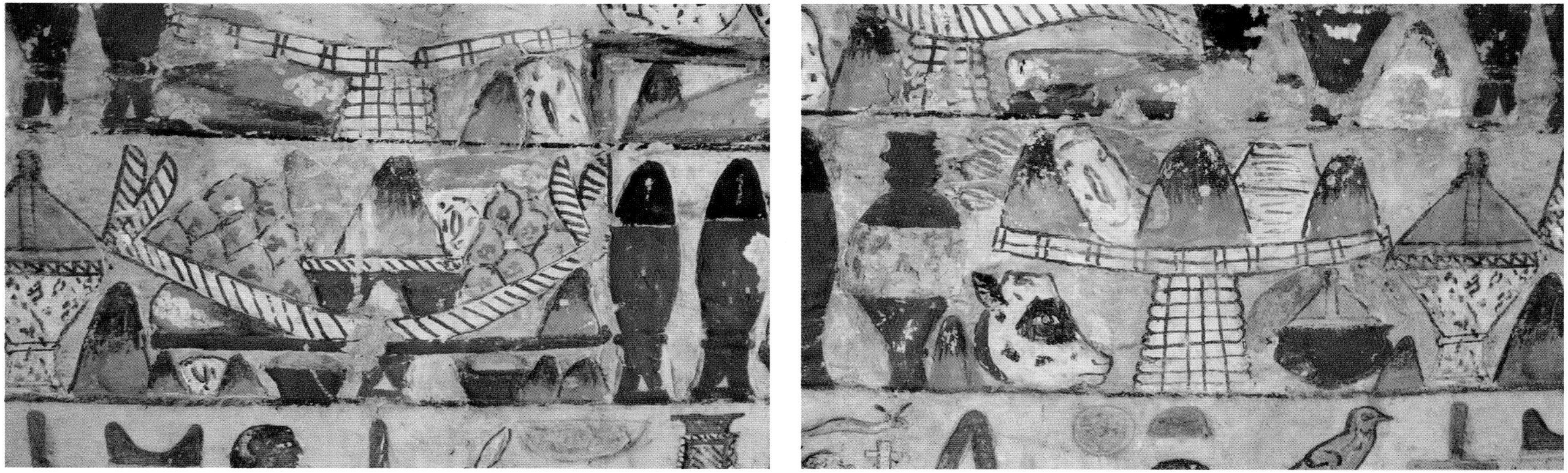

(a) South, upper part, details

(b) Hieroglyphs, details

East wall

(a) Statues 1 to 5

(b) Statues 3 and 4

East wall, north

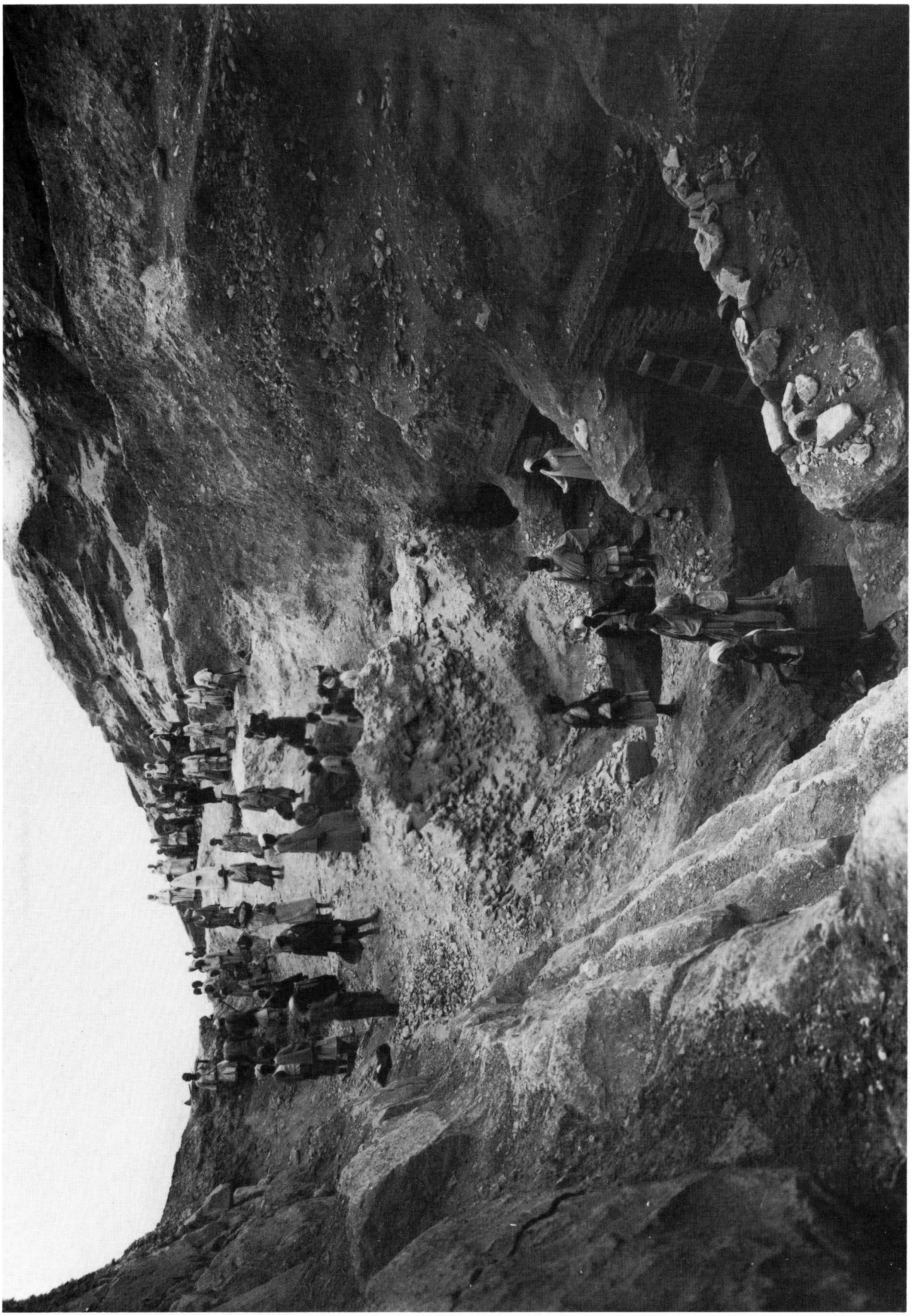

Original excavations south of Unis causeway 1939-40, looking east

(a) Present access to tomb of Irukaptah, looking west to Unis pyramid

(b) Entrance details

Pl. 7. Court and entrance to offering chamber

North and east walls, looking north

(a) Upper part

(b) Detail

Pl. 9. North wall

(b) Registers 3 and 4

(a) Registers 1 and 2

Pl. 10. East wall, north end, lower part

East wall, north end, upper part

Pl. 11.

Pl. 12. East wall, north end, upper part, details

East wall, north, upper part

Pl. 13.

Pl. 14. East wall, north, upper part, details

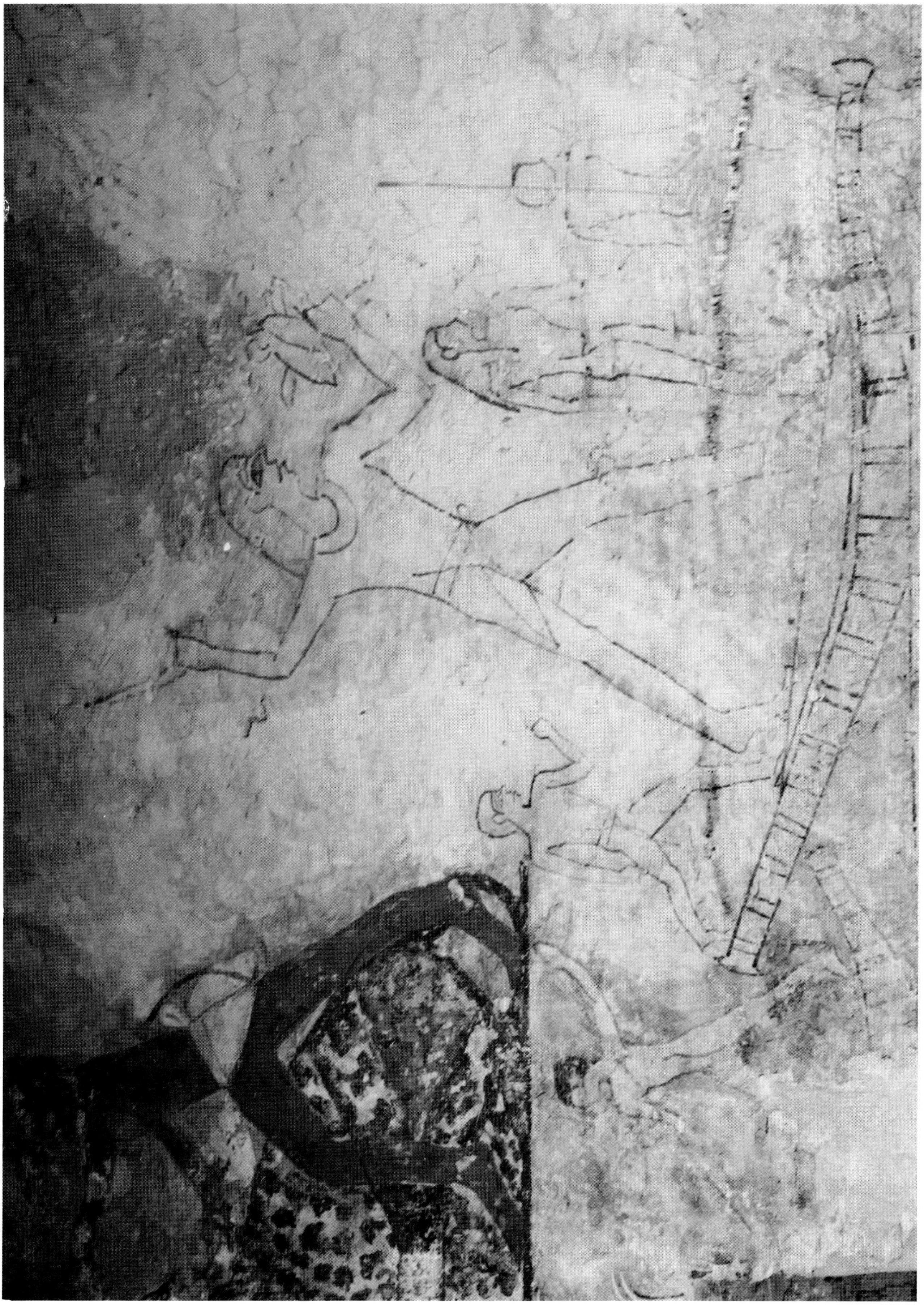

East wall, centre, upper part

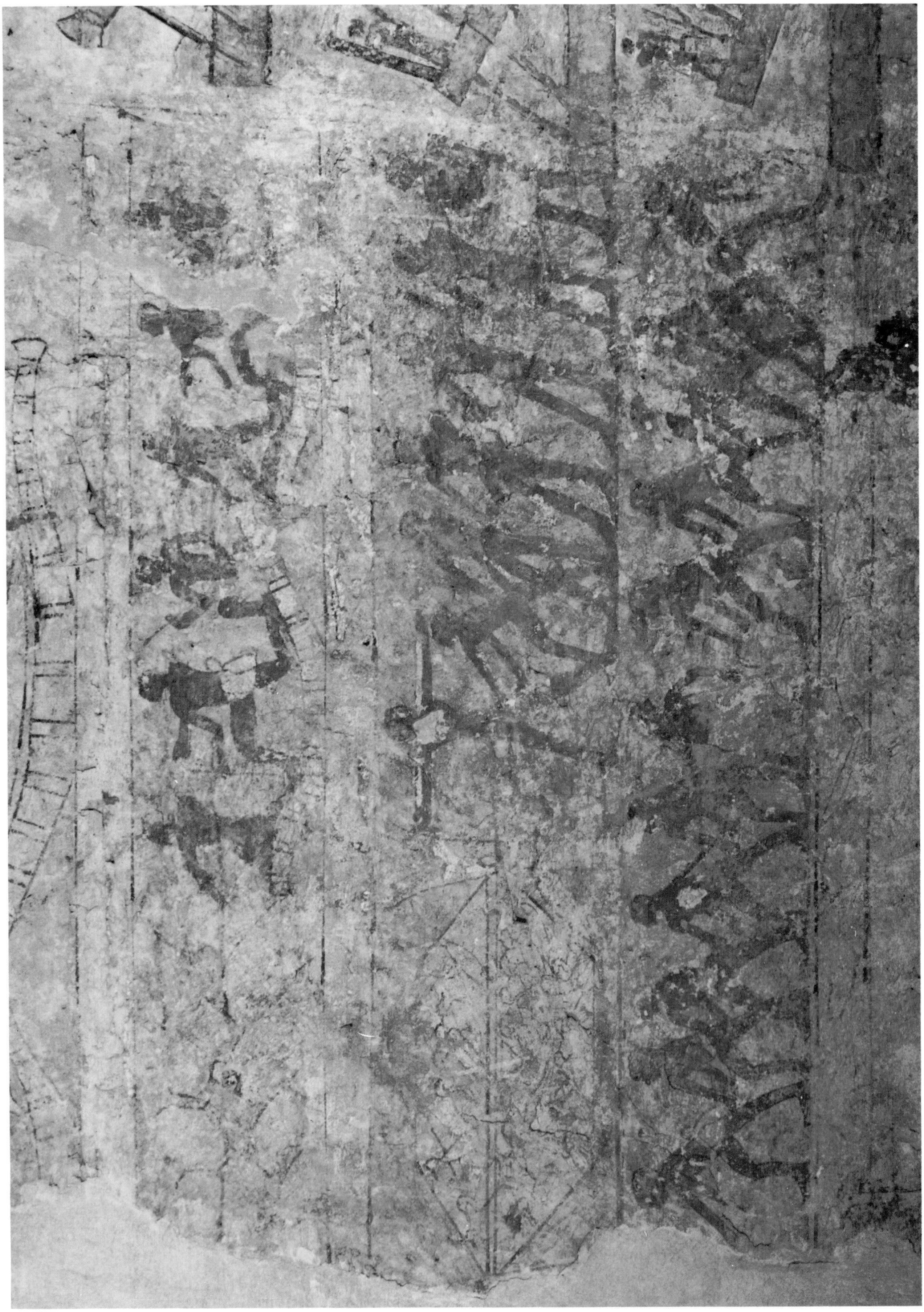

East wall, centre, lower part

Pl. 16.

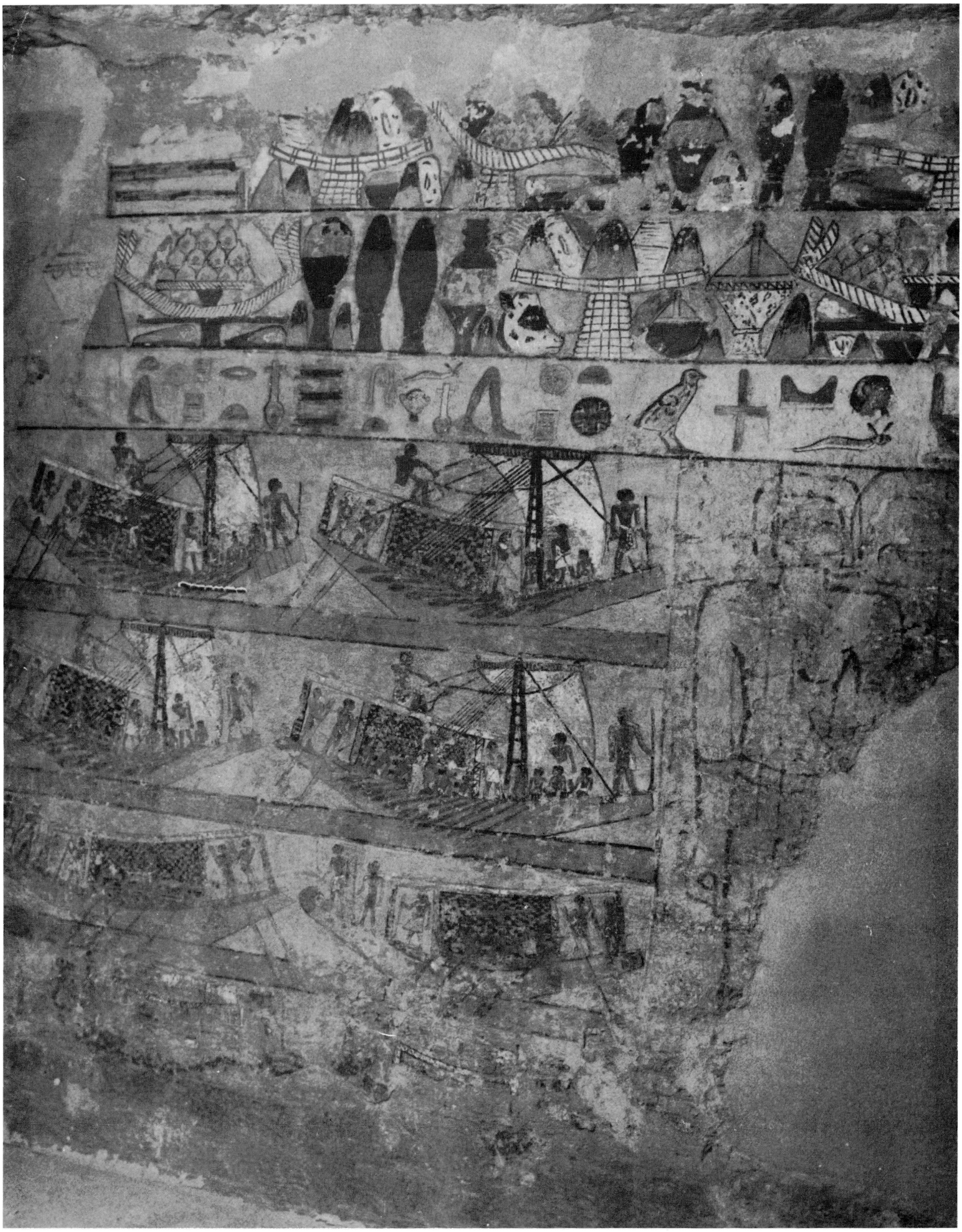

Pl. 17. East wall, south (left)

(a) Register 1, left

(b) Register 2, right

(c) Register 3, right

(d) Register 4, left

East wall, south, lower part, details

Pl. 19. East wall, south (right)

East wall, south, upper part, detail

Pl. 20.

Pl. 21. East wall, south end

Pl. 22. West wall, false door

Pl. 23. West wall, false door, detail

North and east walls, statues 1 - 10

2 1

Pl. 25. East wall, statues 1 and 2

4 3

Pl. 26. East wall, statues 3 and 4

Pl. 27. East wall, statues 3 and 4 at time of discovery

6 5

Pl. 28. East wall, statues 5 and 6

8 7

Pl. 29. East wall, statues 7 and 8

10 9

Pl. 30. North wall, statues 9 and 10

West wall, looking north, statues 1-4

Pl. 32. West wall, statue 1

Pl. 33. West wall, statue 2

Pl. 34. West wall, statue 3

Pl. 35. West wall, statue 4

(a) East wall, statue 3

(b) West wall, statue 2

Pl. 36. Statue details

West wall, looking south

Pl. 37.

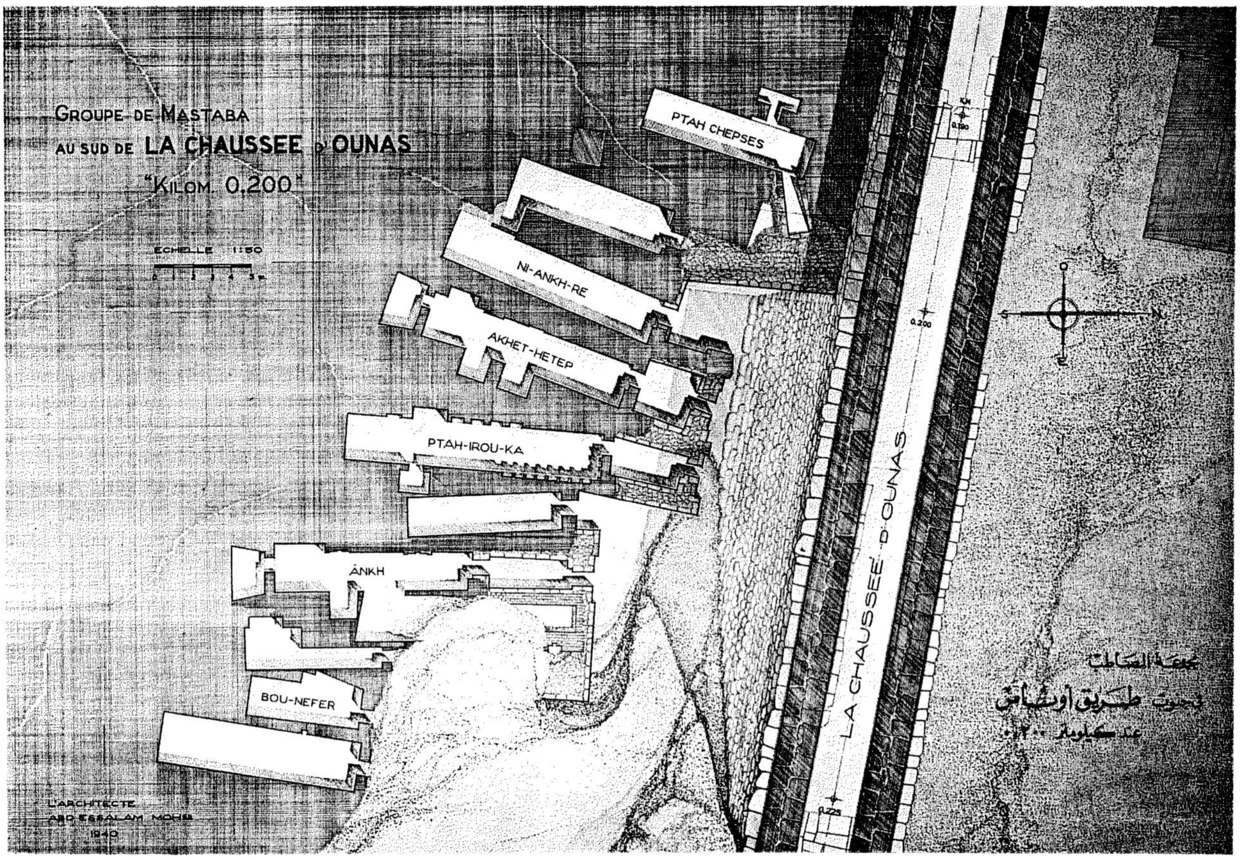

(a) Site map of tombs south of Unis causeway, Abd el-Salam Mohammed Hussein

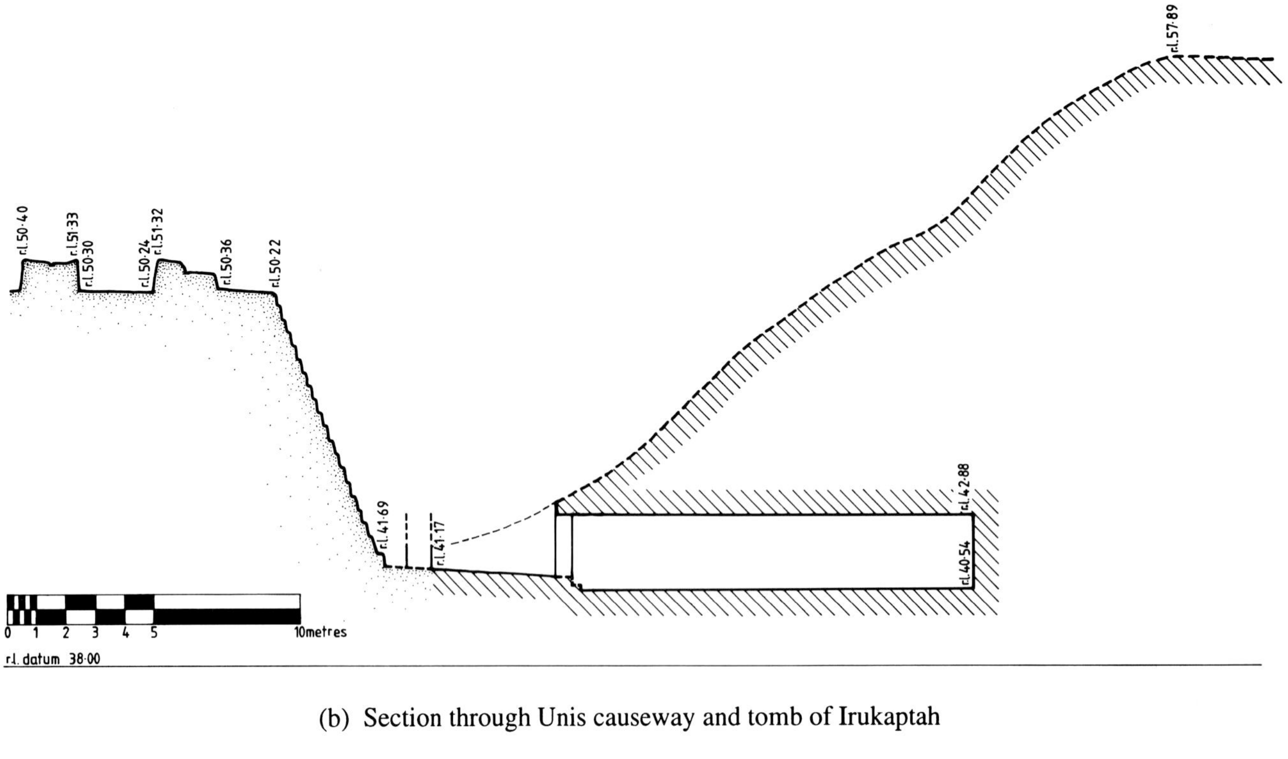

(b) Section through Unis causeway and tomb of Irukaptah

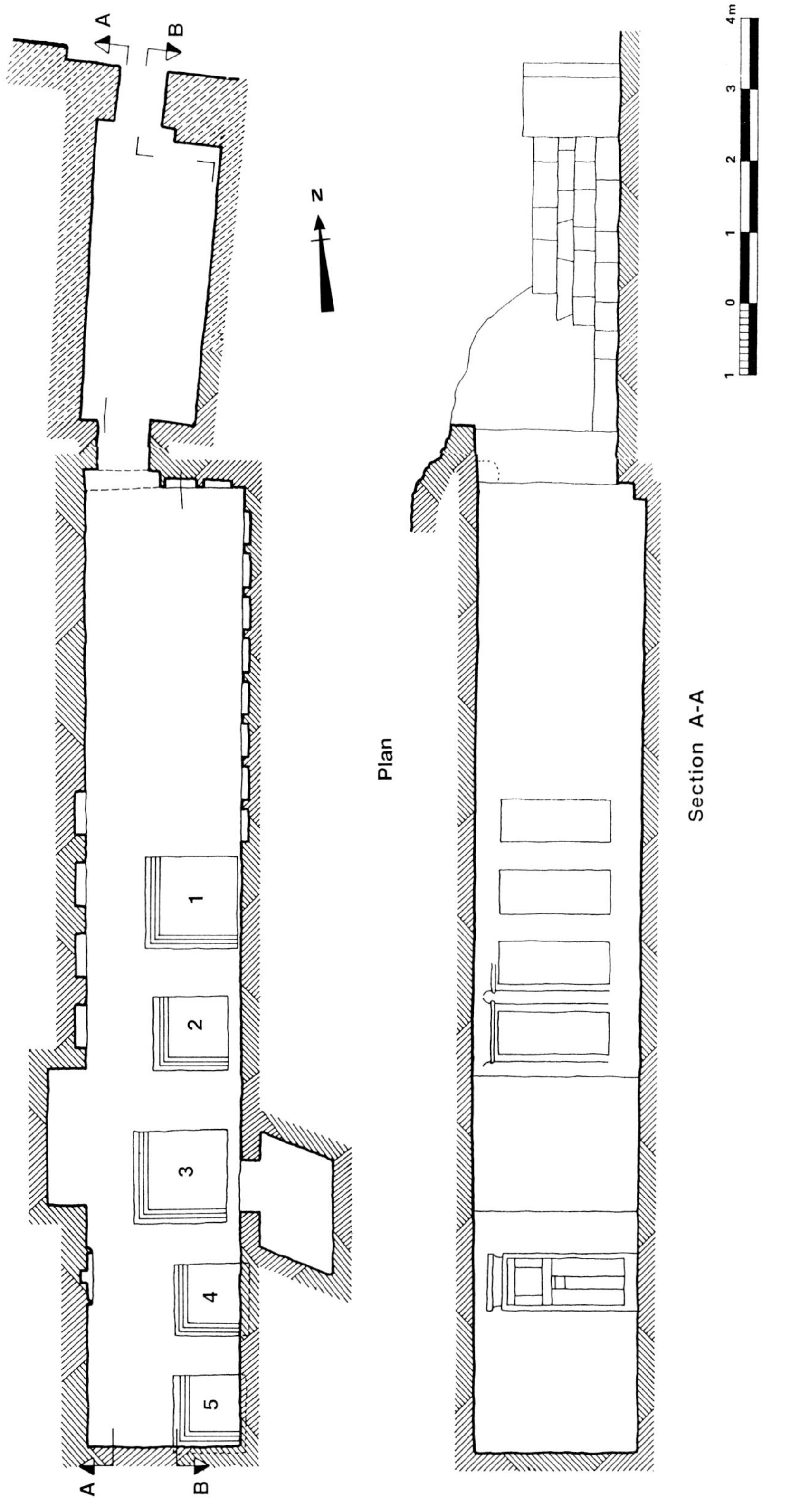

Architectural plan and section

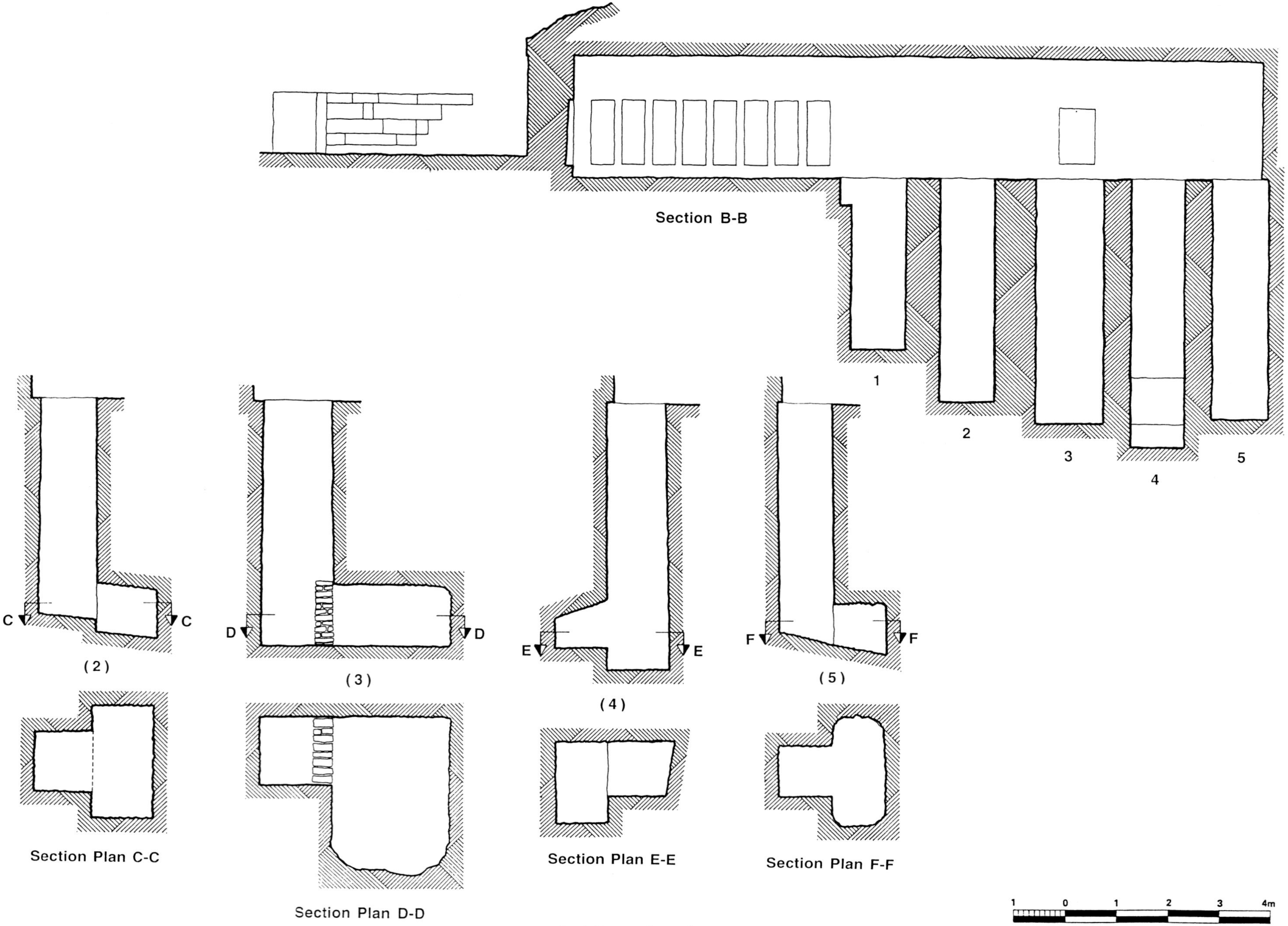

Architectural sections

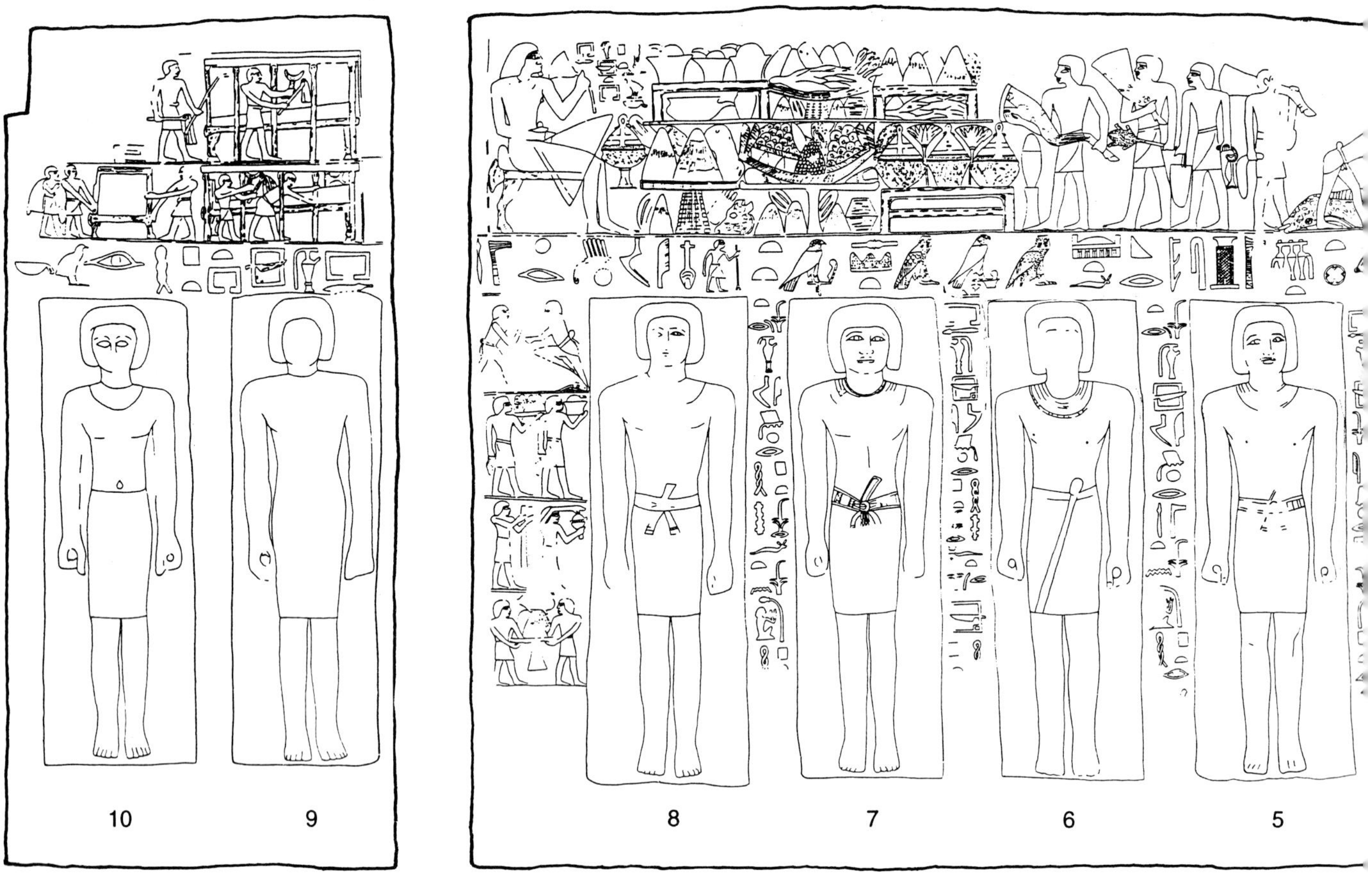

NORTH WALL

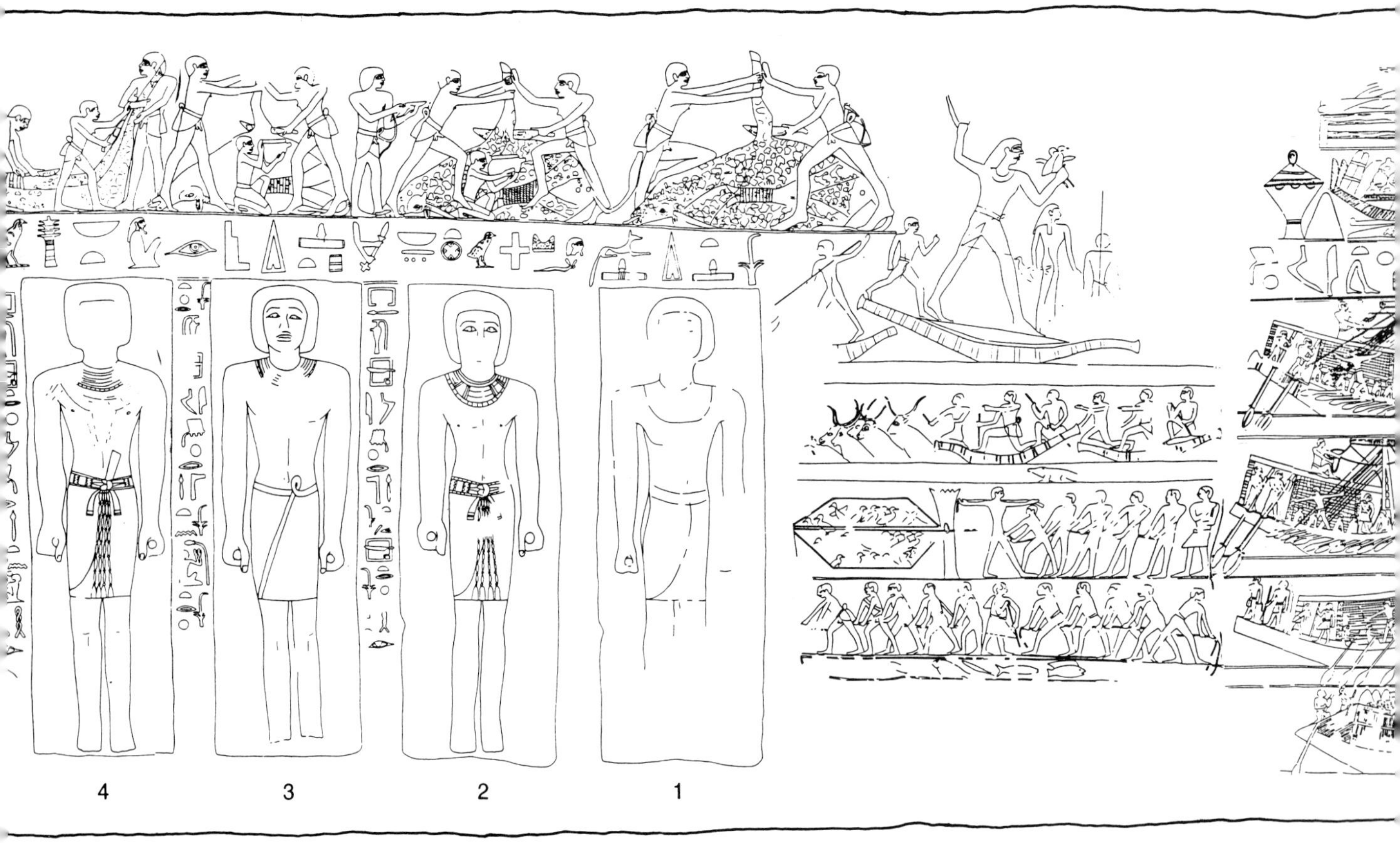

East Wall

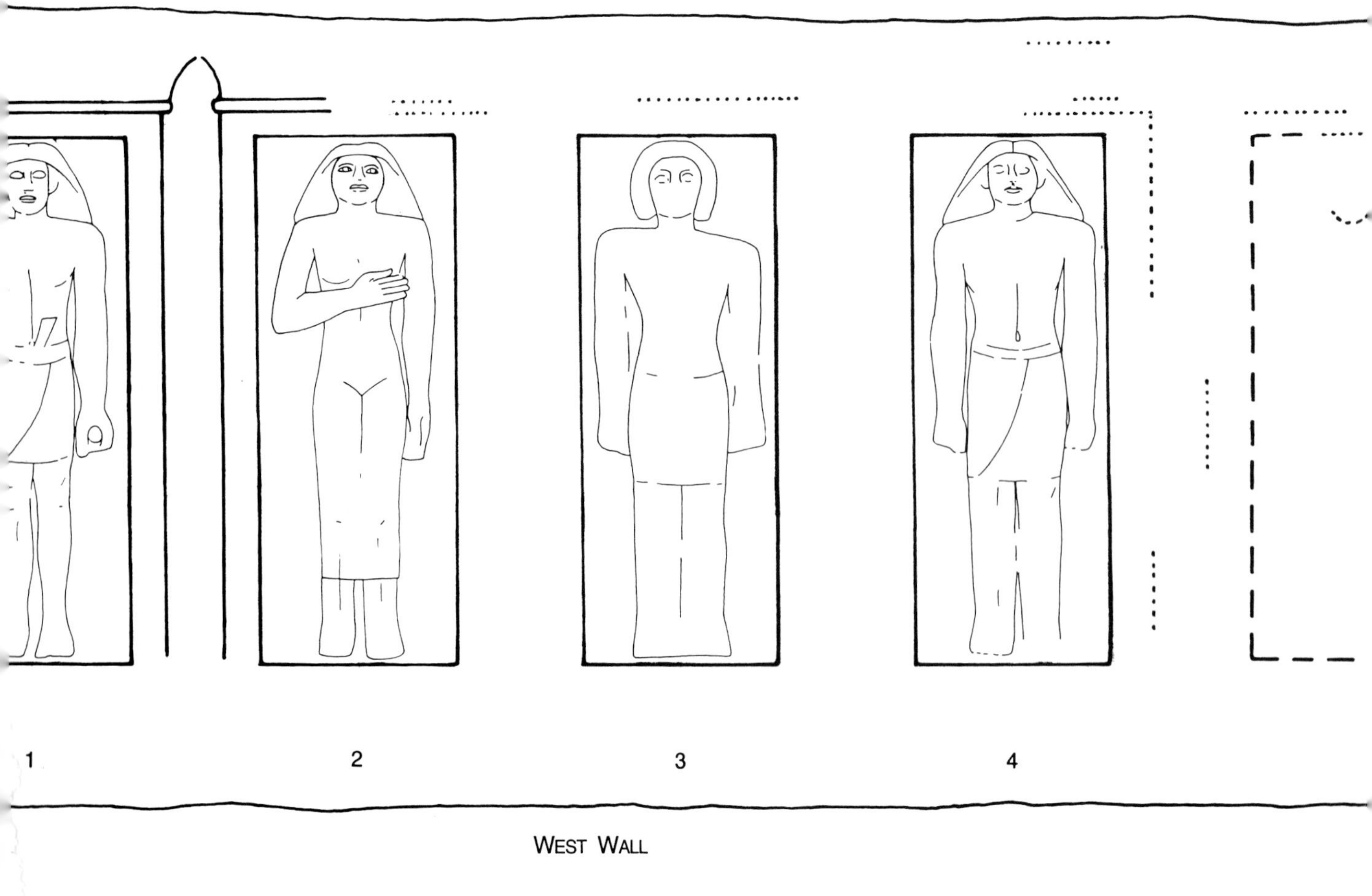

West Wall

Pl. 41. Overview of the offering chapel

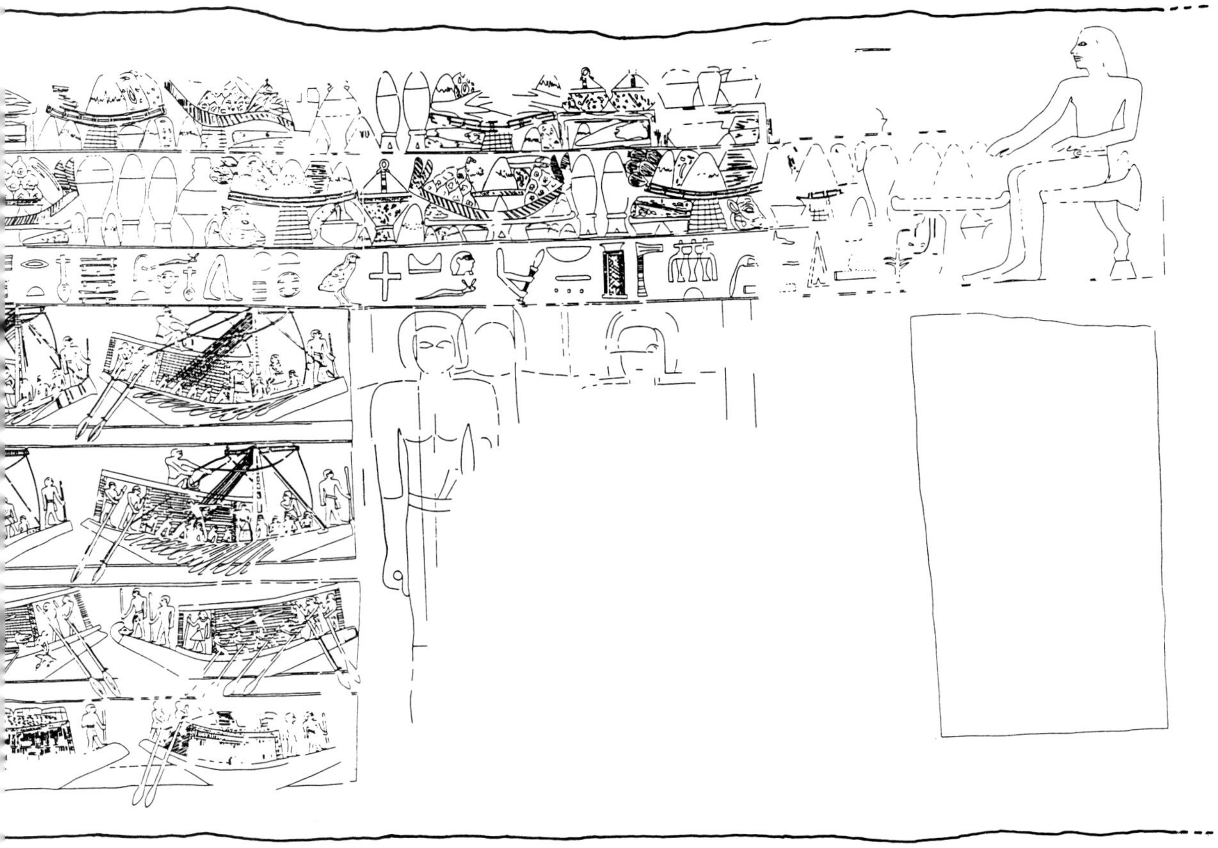

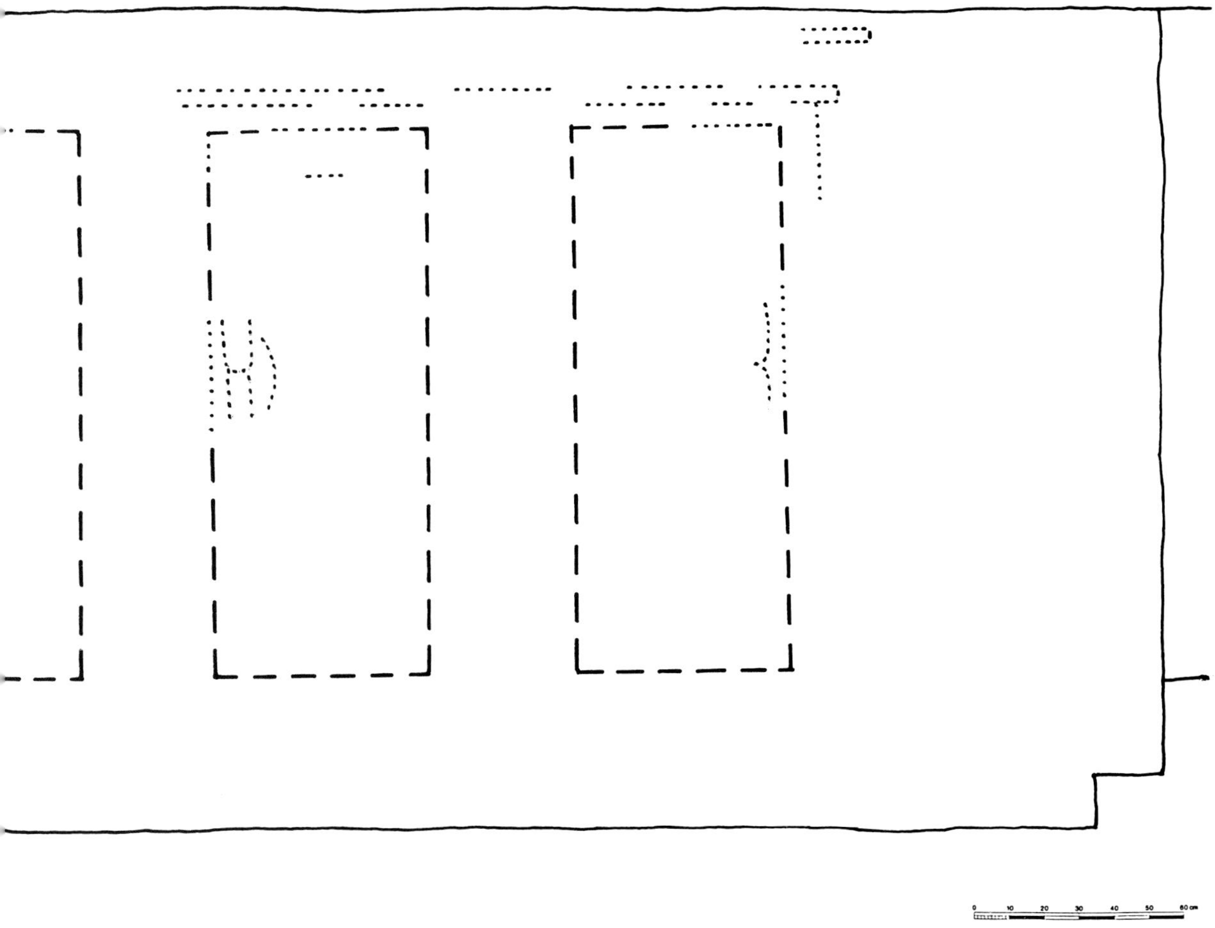
0 10 20 30 40 50 60 cm

Pl. 42. North wall

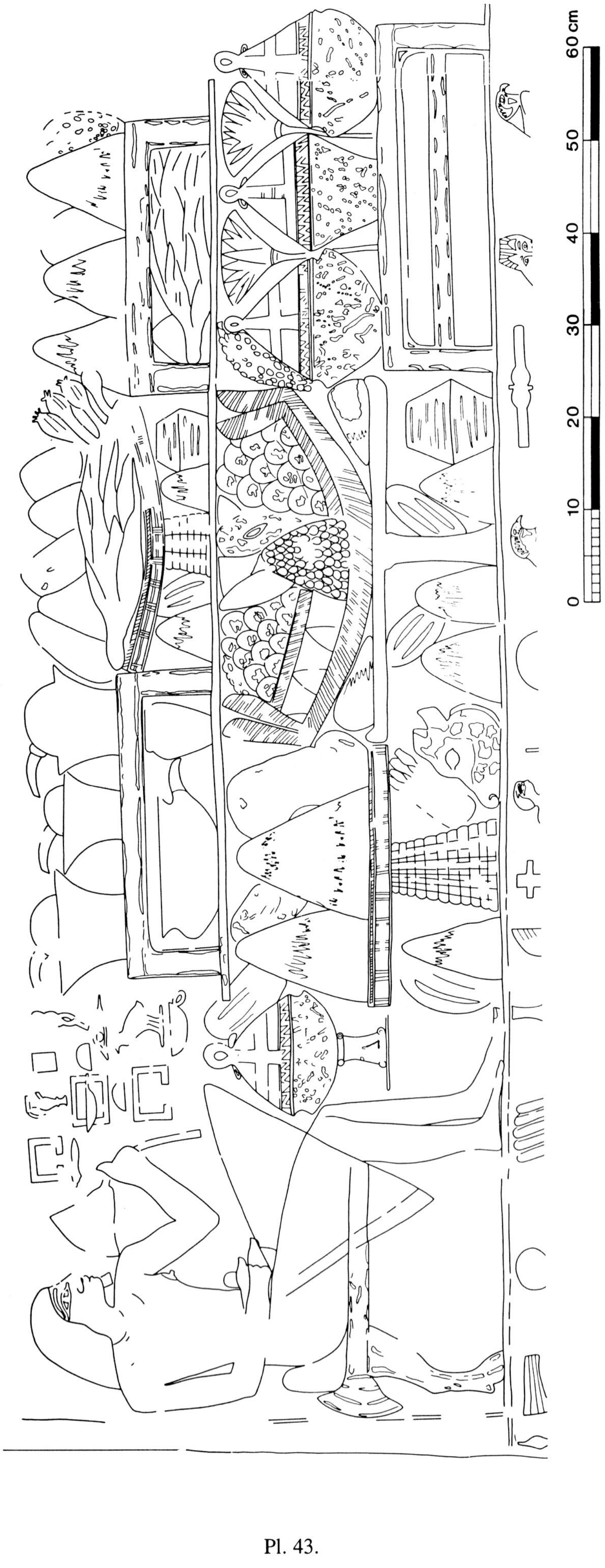

East wall, north end, upper part, detail

45. East wall, north

Pl. 44. East wall

north end

Pl

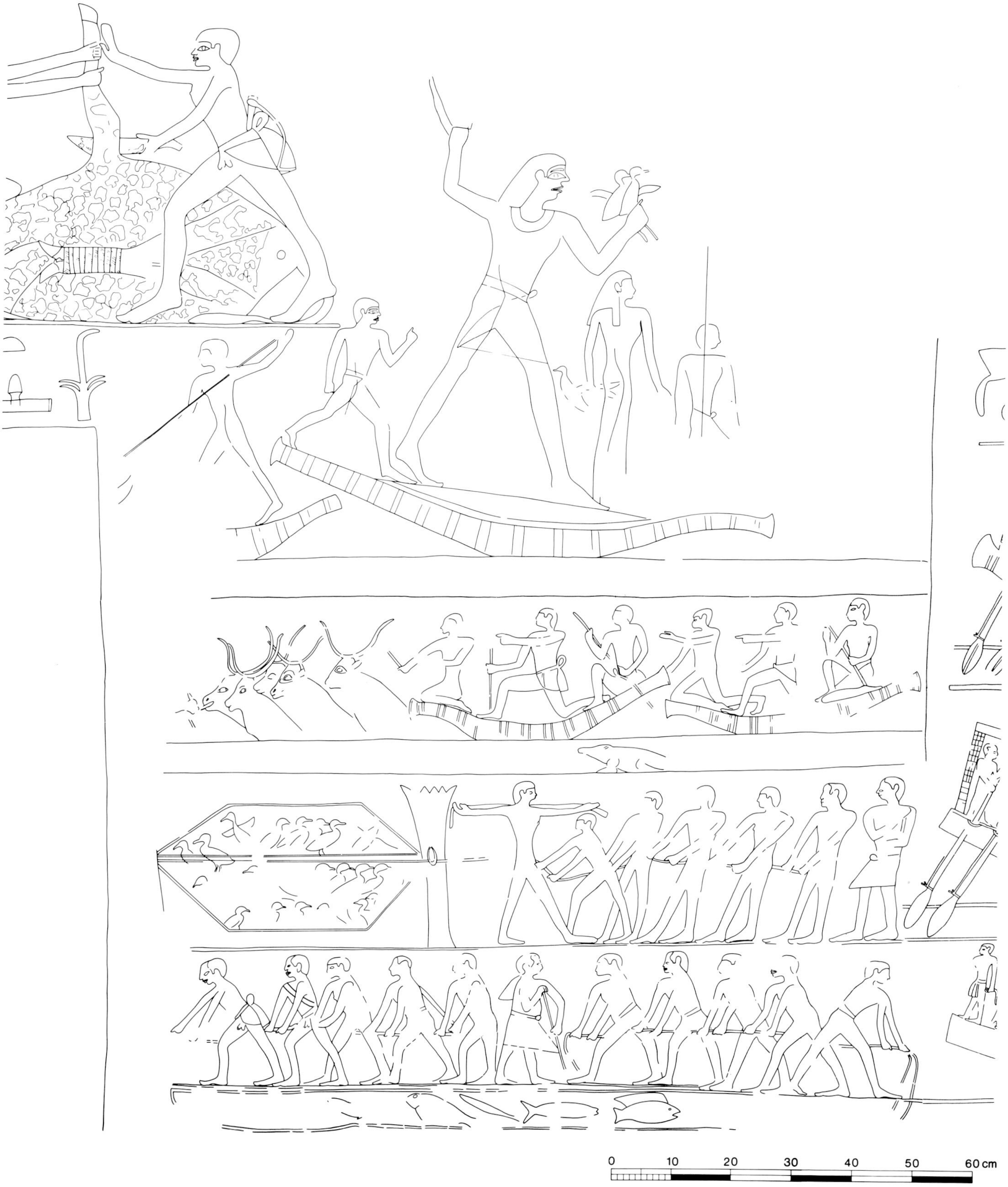

Pl. 46. East wall, centre

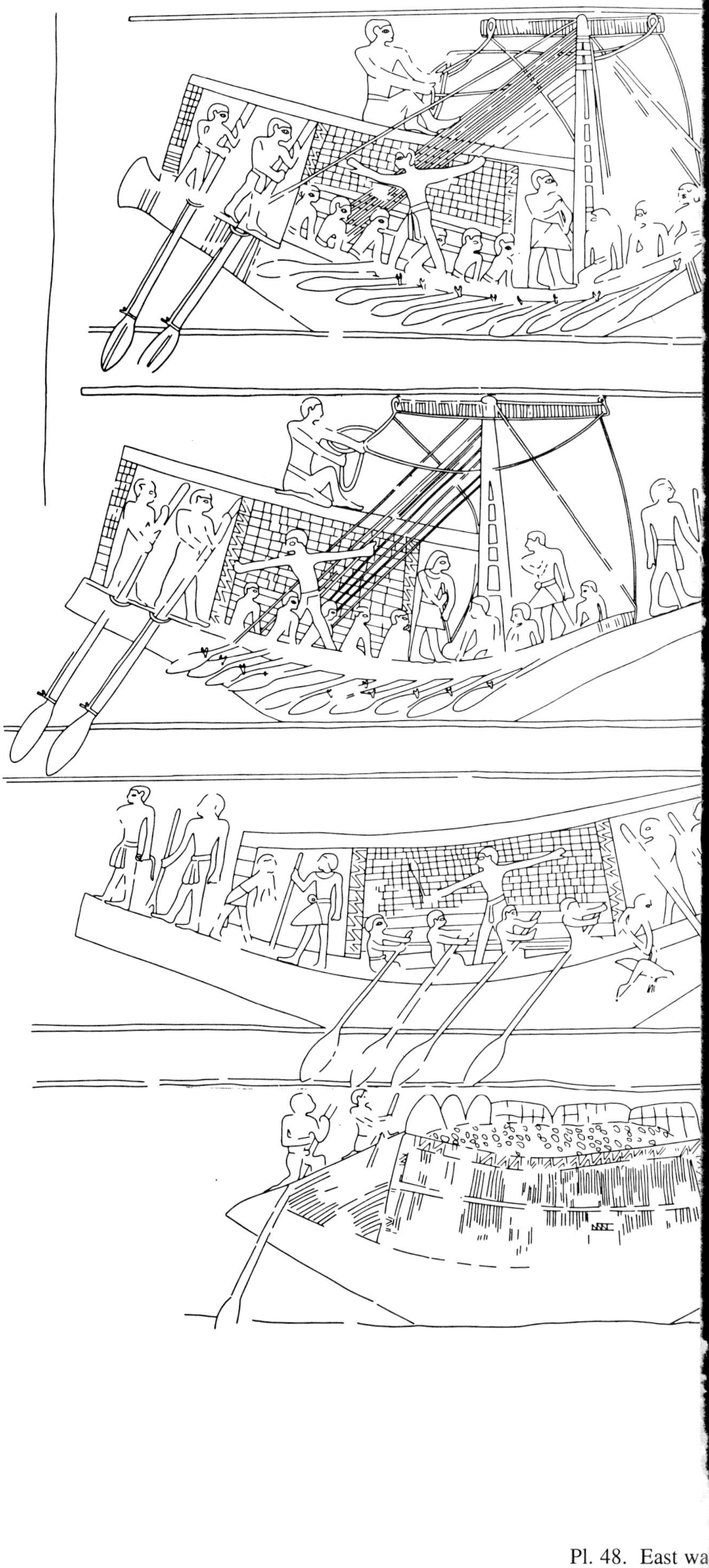

Pl. 48. East wa

all, south

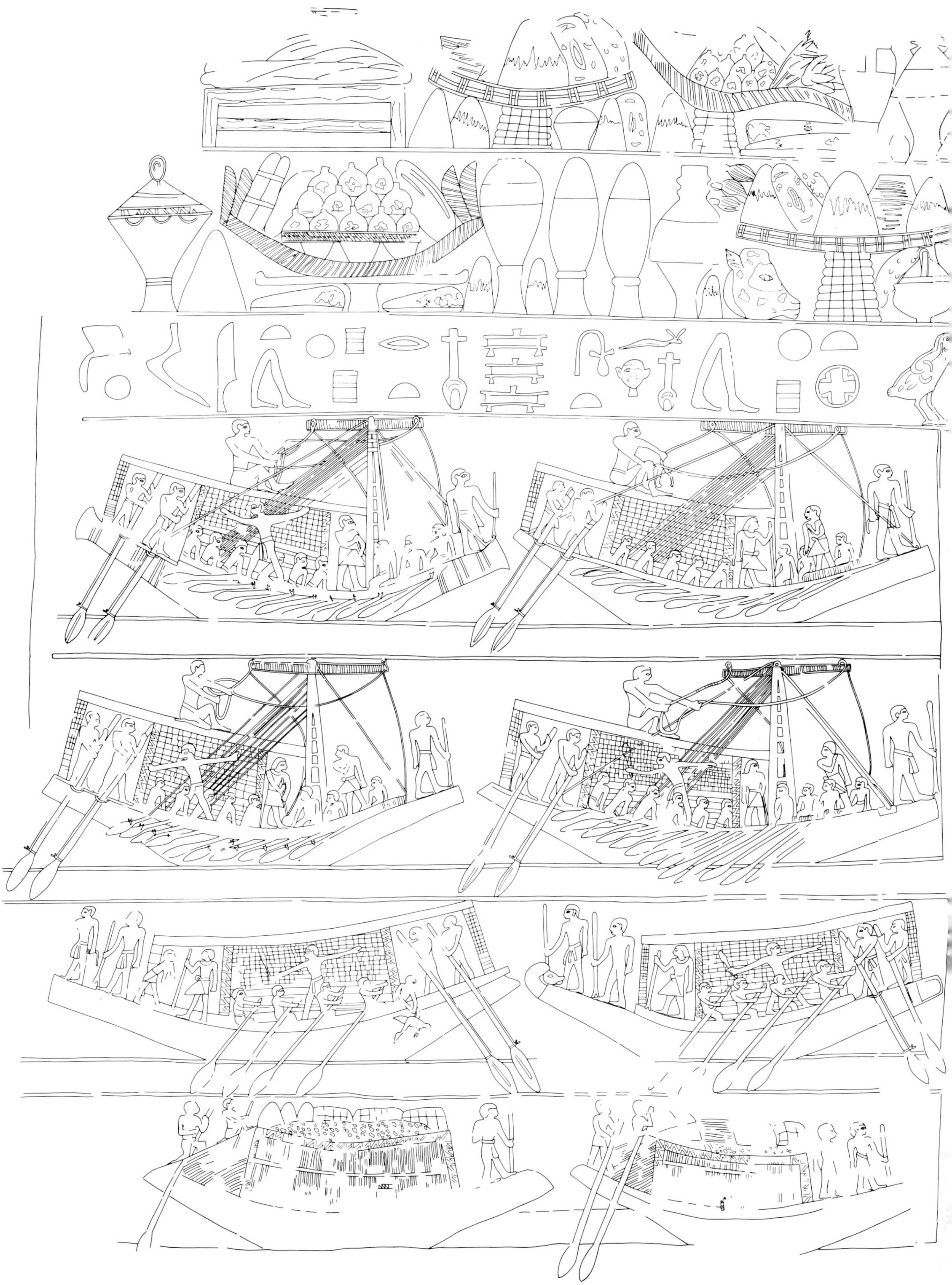

Pl. 47. East w

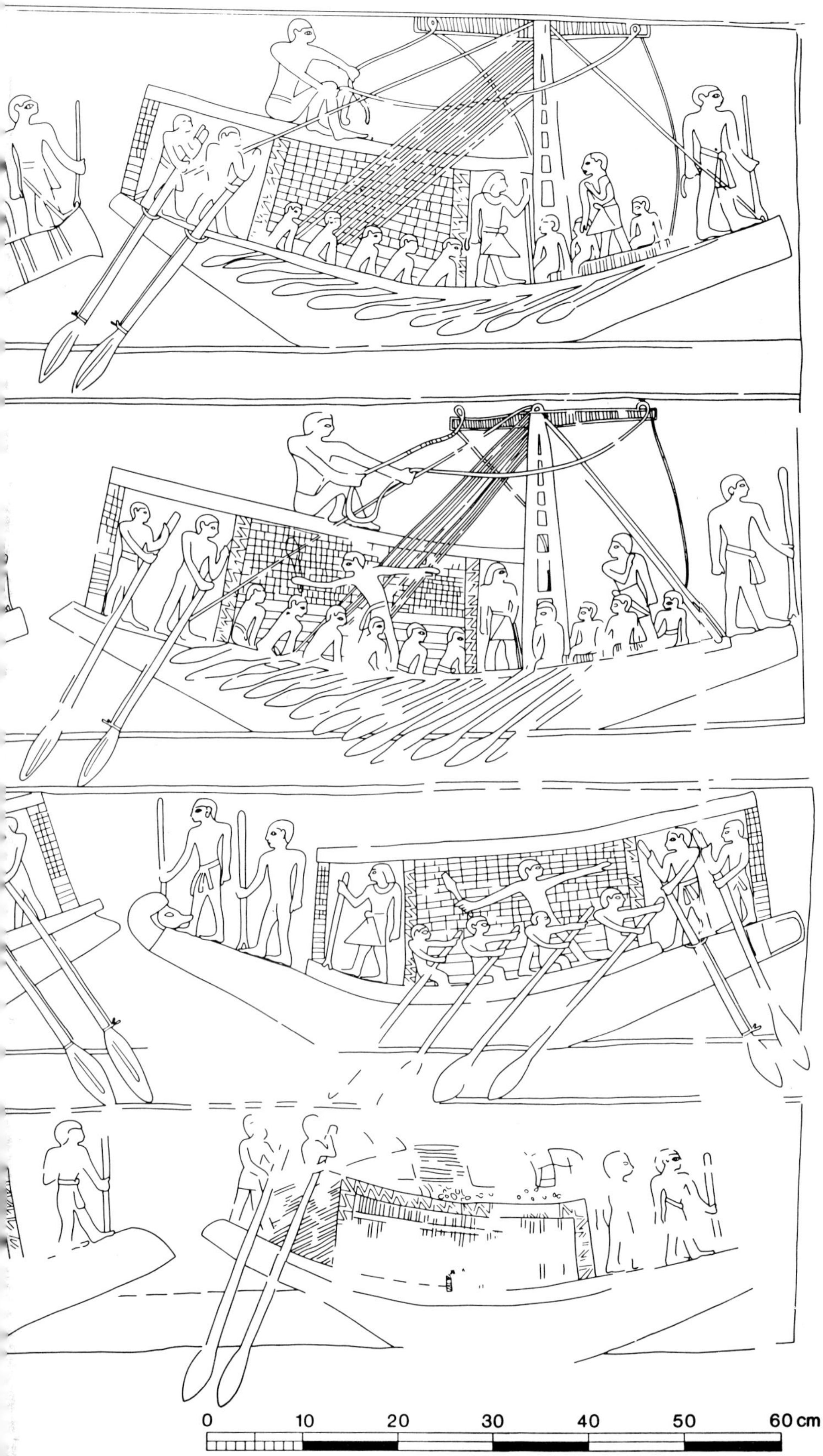

l, south, lower part, detail

Pl. 49. East wall, south end

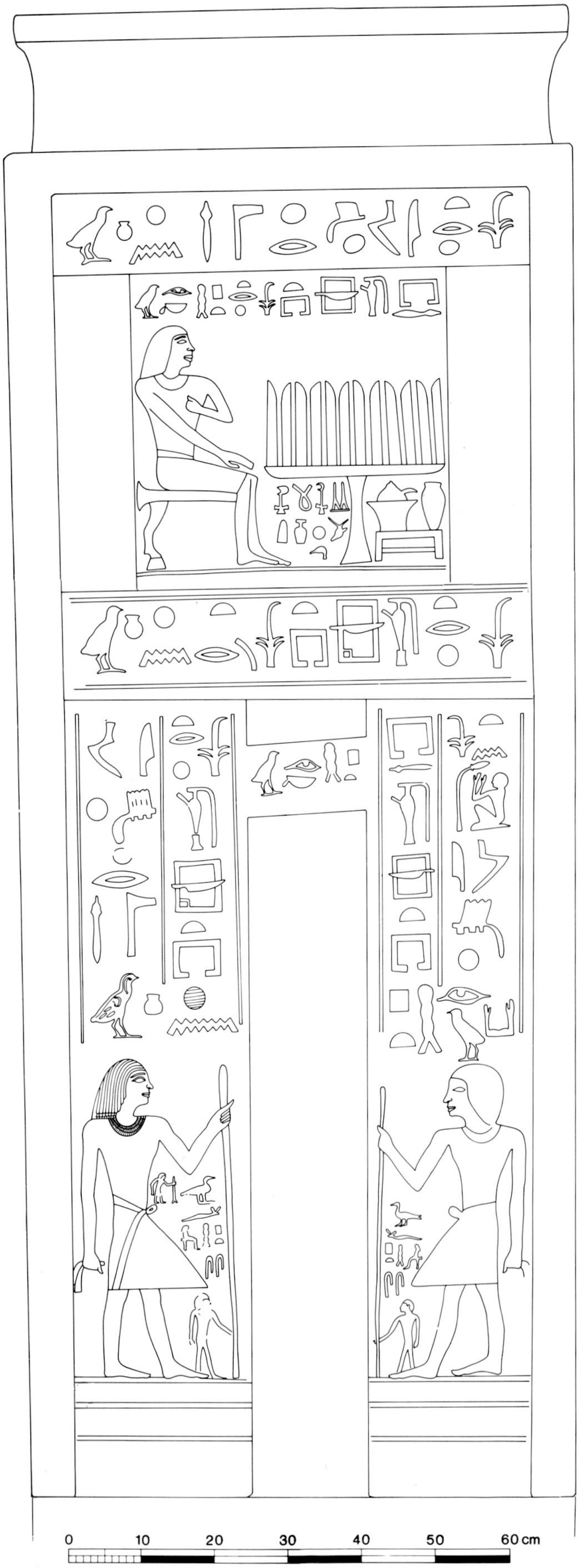

Pl. 50. West wall, false door